The Broadman
MINISTER'S MANUAL

■

Franklin M. Segler

BROADMAN PRESS • Nashville, Tennessee

To my students and

other fellow ministers

© Copyright 1969 • BROADMAN PRESS
Nashville, Tennessee
All rights reserved
ISBN:0-8054-2307-9
4223-07

DEWEY DECIMAL CLASSIFICATION NUMBER: 264
Library of Congress Catalog Card Number: 67-22034
Printed in the United States of America

Preface

Young ministers often ask, "How should I proceed in conducting a formal wedding?" Or, "What is the proper procedure in a funeral service?" Or, "Tell me how to proceed in the ordination of deacons." Or, "Could you suggest an order of worship for a small church which will provide good discipline without being too stiff and formal?" This manual is meant to provide just that kind of help. Its purpose is to provide aid for ministers and others responsible for leading in worship, administering church ordinances, ministering to the sick, and for a general visitation ministry and counseling. Church members generally may also find it helpful in understanding worship and as a guide in private and family devotions.

The manual is meant to be used as a companion to the Bible and the hymnbook. It alone may be adequate for use in certain services, such as in some weddings and funerals, but is not meant to be a substitute for the Bible. Additional passages are usually suggested which may be read from the Bible itself. Several versions of the Bible are used and are designated.

The book is outlined by sections so that the materials desired may be easily located. At the beginning of each chapter certain guiding principles are set forth as practical aids in approaching a particular area of ministry. In many churches it is understood that ministers are not

iii

bound to any particular ritual. It is suggested that the individual minister study these principles and orders of service, together with other resource materials, and then plan his own order of service. By following this procedure, the minister has the treasures of Christian history as resources, and at the same time he may use his own creative imagination in making his ministry contemporary and relevant.

No particular originality is claimed for this manual. Many resources have been drawn upon in this production. The aim has been to make it as contemporary in language and spirit as possible.

This manual of services has grown out of a background of over twenty years of ministry in local churches and sixteen years of teaching young ministers in the seminary. I have attempted to produce the kind of practical manual that was desired for my own ministry through the years. Actually, it has been approximately twenty years in the making. I am indebted to many pastors as well as colleagues in the teaching ministry for many of these materials. With this brief introduction and explanation, the manual is offered with a prayer that fellow ministers in the Lord may find it helpful and that God may see fit to place his blessings upon its ministry.

FRANKLIN M. SEGLER

Contents

Part I

Orders for Public Worship

The chief end of man is to glorify God in worship and in dedicated service. The primary ministry of the church is public worship. In worship man receives vision, inspiration, guidance, and strength for living the dedicated life. Worship is both private and corporate. The individual Christian brings his own contribution to corporate worship and in turn receives additional edification and strength from his fellow worshipers.

In the Bible, worship is presented as the disciplined activity of God's people as they adore him and celebrate his acts in history. Although worship is a direct conscious experience between God and man, this experience is mediated by certain objective elements. God mediates his revelation to man through his words and his actions. Man responds with words and acts through a certain orderliness in public worship.

Guiding Principles

1. Order and spontaneity are linked in the church's worship of God. Suggested orders are meant to be aids and not rigid restrictions. God the Holy Spirit moves as he will in the experiences of men. Men are free to respond to God in a spontaneous manner.

2. Worship is a dialogue between God and man. God

takes the initiative and man responds. Then as man comes for public worship he acts toward God and God responds to him.

3. The act of worship includes adoration and praise, thanksgiving, confession, petitions and intercessions, and active commitment in service. In Christian worship, recognition of the lordship of Christ is a primary goal of the church.

4. Worship is expressed symbolically through words, actions, music, and other art forms. The various means for expressing worship are the reading of the Scriptures, the singing of hymns and anthems, the offering of prayers, the proclamation of the gospel of grace, and the presentation of offerings, including material things and the lives of God's people. The Scriptures exhort, "Present your bodies as a living sacrifice, holy and acceptable to God, which is your spiritual worship" (see Rom. 12:1,RSV).[1]

The following orders of worship are meant to provide guidelines and not to be used slavishly. These patterns will perhaps suggest to the creative leader other ways and means of planning good orders of worship For example, the prayers included here are not meant to be read, but simply to serve as examples of how various prayers in an order of worship should be expressed. The invocation is a brief introductory prayer inviting people into the presence of God and invoking his blessings upon

---

[1] For a more thorough discussion of the meaning of worship and the planning and leading of worship, see Franklin Segler, *Christian Worship: Its Theology and Practice* (Nashville: Broadman Press, 1967).

them. The pastoral prayer should include thanksgiving, confession, petition, intercession, and commitment.

Two suggested orders of worship are presented here: first, a simple order which may be used in a smaller church without a trained choir; and second, a more elaborate service which may be used in larger churches with trained musicians.

Order of Service (I)

Morning Worship
February 26, 1967
10:50 A.M.

PRELUDE—"God Is Our Salvation" . . . . Bach
CALL TO WORSHIP (by the minister)
"God is spirit, and those who worship him must worship in spirit and truth" (John 4:24, RSV).
HYMN OF PRAISE—"Holy, Holy, Holy" . . . . Dykes
INVOCATION
O Lord, God of grace and light,
Open our mouths that we may show forth thy praise;
Enlighten our minds that we may understand thy truth;
Bestow thy grace upon our hearts that we may be dedicated for thy service,
In the name of Christ our Lord. Amen.
HYMN OF DEVOTION—
"Saviour, Like a Shepherd Lead Us" . . . Bradbury
WELCOME TO GUESTS
THE READING OF THE
WORD OF GOD . . . . Responsive Reading
(May be read by the minister, or by the minister and

the congregation in unison, or responsively by the minister and the congregation)

PASTORAL PRAYER (thanksgiving, confession, petition, and intercession)

ANTHEM (by the choir; solo, duet, or other special music)

OFFERTORY SENTENCE

"Every good endowment and every perfect gift is from above, coming down from the Father of lights with whom there is no variation or shadow due to change" (James 1:17, RSV).

Let us now worship God with our tithes and offerings.

OFFERTORY—

"All Creatures of Our God and King" . . . . Rohlig

PRESENTATION OF TITHES AND OFFERINGS AND

OFFERTORY PRAYER

HYMN OF AFFIRMATION—

"I Love Thy Kingdom, Lord" . . . . . . Williams

SERMON—"God's Glorious Church" . . . The Pastor

HYMN OF DEDICATION—

"Take My Life and Let It Be" . . . . . . Bradbury

RECEPTION OF NEW MEMBERS

BENEDICTION

POSTLUDE—"All Glory, Laud, and Honor" . . Bender

Order of Service (II)

Morning Worship
February 26, 1967
10:50 A.M.

SACRED ORGAN MUSIC—"Chorale" . . . . . . Scheidt
(Enter and pray.)

THE SERVICE OF PRAISE

PROCESSIONAL HYMN—
"When Morning Gilds the Skies" . . . . . . Barnby

CALL TO WORSHIP

CHOIR:	Shout and sing for joy, for great in your midst is the holy One of Israel.
CONGREGATION:	For he is our God; and we are the people of his pasture, and the sheep of his hand.
MINISTER:	Today if ye will hear his voice, harden not your heart.

INVOCATION

* * *

THE SERVICE OF PRAYER

PASTOR'S PARAGRAPH

THE READING OF THE SCRIPTURES—John 19:23–27
(The congregation will rise and remain standing through the Gloria Patri.)

GLORIA PATRIA

SILENT MEDITATION

MORNING PRAYER

* * * THE SERVICE OF PROCLAMATION

CHILDREN'S SERMON (if desired)

ANTHEM—
"Blessed Man Whom God Doth Aid". . . . Lovelace
The Carol Choirs

MORNING OFFERING
Offertory—
"As Jesus Stood Beside the Cross" . . . . Scheidt
The Prayer of Dedication

ANTHEM—"Sanctus" . . . . Gounod
  Holy, holy, Lord God Almighty, holy, holy, Lord God
  of Sabaoth. Heaven and earth show Thy glory, heaven
  and earth are full of Thy glory. Glory and pow'r be
  Thine forever. Glory be to Thy Holy name. Hosanna
  in the highest. Amen.
SERMON—"Those Who Loved Him" . . . The Pastor

THE SERVICE OF PROFESSION

HYMN OF DEDICATION—
  "When I Survey the Wondrous Cross" . . . Mason
RECEPTION OF NEW MEMBERS
BENEDICTION AND CHORAL AMEN
ORGAN DISMISSAL
***Ushers will assist with seating at these periods.

Resources for Worship Services

In planning the worship services the minister should
make use of all the resources available. He should seek
to avoid repetition and monotony in the services week
after week. The opening sentences of the service or the
call to worship, the invocation or opening prayer, the
responsive readings, the offertory sentences and offertory prayer, and the benedictions provide opportunity
for both discipline and variety in the services. The few
suggestions which follow may serve as examples of other
selections which the creative minister may formulate
and select. No example of the pastoral prayer is given
here due to its length. This prayer, sometimes considered the main prayer or the long prayer of the service,
includes prayers of thanksgiving, confession, petition,

and intercession. A manual of prayers such as Noyes's *Prayers for Services* will provide many suggestions for the pastoral prayer.

Calls to Worship

Serve the Lord with gladness: come before his presence with singing. . . . Enter into his gates with thanksgiving, and into his courts with praise: be thankful unto him, and bless his name. For the Lord is good; his mercy is everlasting; and his truth endureth to all generations [*Psalm 100:2–5, KJV*].

Ascribe to the Lord the glory of his name; worship the Lord in holy array [*Psalm 29:2, RSV*].

I will bless the Lord at all times: his praise shall continually be in my mouth. . . . O magnify the Lord with me, and let us exalt his name together! [*Psalm 34:1–3, KJV*].

O come, let us worship and bow down: let us kneel before the Lord our maker. For he is our God; and we are the people of his pasture, and the sheep of his hand [*Psalm 95:6–7, KJV*].

Come unto me, all ye that labour and are heavy laden, and I will give you rest. Take my yoke upon you, and learn of me; for I am meek and lowly in heart: and ye shall find rest unto your souls [*Matt. 11:28–29, KJV*].

I was glad when they said to me, "Let us go to the house of the Lord!" [*Psalm 122:1, RSV*].

I lift up my eyes to the hills. From whence does my help come? My help comes from the Lord, who made heaven and earth [*Psalm 121:1–2, RSV*].

They that wait upon the Lord shall renew their strength; they shall mount up with wings as eagles; they shall run and not be weary; and they shall walk, and not faint [*Isa. 40:31, KJV*].

Invocations

(1) Almighty God, unto whom all hearts are open, all desires known, and from whom no secrets are hid, cleanse the thoughts of our hearts by the inspiration of thy Holy Spirit, that we may perfectly love thee, and worthily magnify thy holy name; through Jesus Christ our Lord. Amen. (From an ancient book of worship.)

(2) Almighty and everlasting God, in whom we live and move and have our being, grant to us purity of heart and strength of purpose, so that we may seek thy will and do it without faltering; for the sake of Jesus Christ, thy Son. Amen.

Offertory Sentences

Every good endowment and every perfect gift is from above, coming down from the Father of lights with whom there is no variation or shadow due to change [*James 1:17, RSV*].

Remember the words of the Lord Jesus, . . . It is more blessed to give than to receive [*Acts 20:35, KJV*].

Bless the Lord, O my soul: and all that is within me, bless his holy name. Bless the Lord, O my soul, and forget not all his benefits [*Psalm 103:1–2, KJV*].

What shall I render unto the Lord for all his benefits toward me? . . . I will pay my vows unto the Lord now in the presence of all his people [*Psalm 116:12–14,KJV*].

Upon the first day of the week let every one of you lay by him in store, as God hath prospered him [*1 Cor. 16:2,KJV*].

For you know the grace of our Lord Jesus Christ, that though he was rich, yet for your sake he became poor, so that by his poverty you might become rich [*2 Cor. 8:9,RSV*].

Offertory Prayers

(1) O Lord, our Heavenly Father, who hast freely given us all things through Jesus Christ, accept now these gifts we bring, and give us thy grace, that we may yield ourselves completely unto thee. Use our gifts and our abilities to the honor of thy kingdom. In Jesus' name. Amen.

(2) Gracious Father, as thou hast freely given us all things, we now freely give unto thee ourselves and the substance of our hands. Accept these gifts as a token of our sincere worship of thee. In the name of Christ our Lord. Amen.

(3) O Lord, creator of heaven and earth, and the source of all we are and have, we come to present our tithes and offerings to the glory of thy holy name. We beseech thee graciously to accept and bless our gifts, through Jesus Christ our Lord. Amen.

Benedictions

The Lord bless you and keep you: The Lord make his face to shine upon you, and be gracious to you: The Lord lift up his countenance upon you, and give you peace [*Num. 6:24–26,RSV*].

Grace be unto you, and peace, from God our

Father, and from the Lord Jesus Christ [*1 Cor. 1:3,KJV*].

The grace of the Lord Jesus Christ, and the love of God, and the communion of the Holy Ghost, be with you all. Amen [*2 Cor. 13:14,KJV*].

The peace of God, which passeth all understanding, shall keep your hearts and minds through Christ Jesus. Now unto God and our Father be glory for ever and ever. Amen [*Phil. 4:7,20,KJV*].

Now the God of peace, that brought again from the dead our Lord Jesus, that great shepherd of the sheep, through the blood of the everlasting covenant, make you perfect in every good work to do his will, working in you that which is well-pleasing in his sight, through Jesus Christ; to whom be glory for ever and ever. Amen [*Heb. 13:20–21,KJV*].

Now unto him that is able to keep you from falling, and to present you faultless before the presence of his glory with exceeding joy, to the only wise God our Saviour, be glory and majesty, dominion and power, both now and ever. Amen [*Jude 24–25,KJV*].

The grace of our Lord Jesus Christ be with you all. Amen [*Rev. 22:21,KJV*].

Part II

Baptism and the Lord's Supper

Baptism and the Lord's Supper are considered ordinances of the church given by command of our Lord. They are to be perpetuated as a part of the worship, witness, and mission of the church. They are acts of worship. As God's enacted word they proclaim the gospel. By these acts the individual expresses his personal faith and commitment. The congregation expresses the unity and the fellowship of the church in these common acts of worship.

Baptism and the Lord's Supper symbolize great truths of the gospel. In baptism the immersion of the believer symbolizes his death to sin and his resurrection to a new life created in his salvation experience. It is an act of commitment to the Lord Jesus Christ. In baptism the believer identifies with Jesus Christ just as in our Lord's baptism he identified with the sinner.

The Lord's Supper symbolizes the death of Jesus Christ on the cross. The bread symbolizes his broken body, and the cup represents his blood shed for the remission of sins. In partaking of these elements the congregation memorializes the death of Christ and expresses hope in his promised return. In addition, the believer commits himself anew to the living Lord who is vitally present with his people as they carry out his command in solemn worship.

Baptism

Guiding Principles

1. The baptistry should be approximately 8 by 5 feet or larger, and the water 40 to 44 inches in depth. A 6-inch step or concrete block along the front of the baptistry may be used for smaller children so that the water will not be too deep for them. A toe bar may be used to prevent the candidate's feet from floating. The water should be heated to body temperature.

2. A church committee composed of two or more laymen and their wives should supervise the preparation of the baptistry and the equipment. They also may assist the candidates as they dress for the ordinance.

3. Equipment such as the minister's baptismal trousers and robe, the candidate's robes, towels, and so forth, should be provided by the church. A white robe for the minister is preferable, although sometimes a black robe is used.

4. The ordinance is usually administered by the pastor or, if the church has no pastor, some other person designated by the church.

5. The manner in which baptism is administered should aid in the spirit of worship. The pastor should master the techniques of the ordinance so as to make it worshipful. Baptism symbolizes the gospel; therefore, the ceremony should be reverent and dignified.

6. Prior to the service the candidates for baptism should be thoroughly instructed as to the meaning of baptism and as to the procedures in the ceremony itself. The minister may give a demonstration as to how the

candidate will stand and indicate each step in the procedure outlined below.

7. Baptism is usually administered during a regular worship service, either morning or evening. It may come toward the beginning of the service after a hymn and a prayer, or toward the end of the service after the sermon and hymn of commitment. It should proceed as an act of worship in keeping with the other parts of the service.

Suggested Procedure

1. At the proper time the minister will proceed into the baptistry. He will read a brief, appropriate passage of Scripture, or have someone else read a passage as he enters the baptistry. The following passages are appropriate: Matthew 3:13–17; 28:18–20; Mark 1:4,7–8; Acts 2:22–24,38–41,42–47; Romans 6:3–5,8–12; Galatians 3:26–27; Colossians 2:12; 3:1–3. Poems, exhortations, running quotations from the Scriptures, and so on detract from the beauty of the symbolic act of baptism. It should be allowed to proclaim its own message.

2. The candidate will proceed into the baptistry. The pastor may offer his hand to steady the candidate and guide him to the proper position.

3. The candidate will clasp his hands across his chest as he has been previously instructed to do. He will hold his head straight with his body as he is lowered into the water. Just before he is lowered he may draw in a breath and hold it until he is raised from the water. He should allow the minister freedom in lowering and raising him.

4. The minister, standing just beside and slightly be-hind the candidate, will grasp the candidate's hands with his left (or right) hand and raise the other hand in a gesture of reverence and repeat the following or a simi-lar formula:

"A____ [candidate's name], in obedience to the com-mands of our Lord Jesus Christ, and upon your confes-sion of faith in him as Saviour and Lord, I baptize you in the name of the Father and of the Son and of the Holy Spirit. Amen."

5. The minister will place his hand at the base of the candidate's neck between his shoulders and lower him slowly into the water until the face is slightly under the surface, then slowly raise the candidate. The minister may take two short steps to the right (or left) as he lowers the candidate. If the candidate is particularly tall, he may, as previously instructed, bend his knees slightly or kneel as he is lowered into the water.

6. The candidate having been raised, the minister will then guide him to the steps leading from the bap-tistry. If there is more than one candidate, the same procedure will be repeated until all are baptized.

7. A prayer of dedication may then be given for the candidates. If the ordinance is administered at the con-clusion of the service, the minister may pronounce the benediction from the baptistry or ask the choir to have a choral benediction.

8. Hymns of praise, devotion, and commitment are appropriate for a service when baptism is administered. The hymns and the sermon need not necessarily be on

the subject of baptism. They may be on the lordship of Christ, on the church, or on any theme of consecration of life and obedient service.

9. If it is necessary to baptize in an outdoor pool or stream, a brief well-balanced service of praise, prayer, scripture reading, and a short sermon may be planned. A committee should carefully explore and select the exact place for baptizing. The water should be at least waist deep. The candidates should face downstream as they are immersed to avoid the water's rushing into their nostrils. A committee of deacons may be asked to assist.

Wherever the service of baptism is held, it should always be conducted in a spirit of reverence and dignity. "If ye then be risen with Christ, seek those things which are above, where Christ sitteth on the right hand of God" (Col. 3:1,KJV).

The Lord's Supper

Guiding Principles

1. It is the Lord's table. Jesus himself instituted the Supper (See Matt. 26:26-30). Therefore, the most appropriate designation is "The Lord's Supper." It memorializes the atoning death of Jesus Christ. It perpetuates the gospel of redeeming grace. It is a celebration, a thanksgiving for Christ's gift to us, an acknowledgment of his living presence in the act of worship.

2. The church received the command to perpetuate the Lord's Supper until he returns. It is a communion of believers with Christ in common worship. The fellowship of believers is experienced in Christ.

3. For the individual worshiper participation in the Lord's Supper is an act of devotion and consecration. The individual should examine his motives in worship, his relationship to Christ, and his relationship to his fellowman.

4. Since the church is commanded to observe the Lord's Supper regularly, the individual Christian will wish to participate regularly. To neglect this privilege is to disobey Christ.

5. The New Testament gives no definite instruction as to the frequency of the observance of the Supper. Churches observe it variously—some weekly, others monthly, and others quarterly. Perhaps no church should observe it less frequently than once each quarter. It is usually observed either in the Sunday morning or Sunday evening worship service. In some churches it is alternated between the morning and evening services. It may be observed at special seasons such as on Good Friday, New Year's Eve, and other occasions.

6. The order of service for the observance of the Lord's Supper should be carefully planned. The Supper should be made a central part of the service and the entire service kept within the usual length of an hour. The order of service should include praise, devotion, and commitment as in the usual well-rounded worship service. Appropriate Scripture verses and hymns and a brief meditation should be planned. These need not necessarily be limited to the theme of the Lord's Supper. The great themes of the cross, the salvation experience, commitment to Christian living, and other related subjects are appropriate. A service comprised entirely of

music and Scripture selections is something desirable on special occasions, such as New Year's Eve. A service of quiet music and meditation may be effective.

7. A committee of deacons and wives are usually elected to prepare the table and the elements for the Lord's Supper. They will arrange the table linen, plates, trays, and glasses. Unleavened bread, prepared especially for this purpose, may be purchased or made by the committee. If unleavened bread is not available, any white bread or crackers cut or broken into small pieces may be used. A good brand of unfermented grape juice is usually preferred for the cup.

8. The deacons and/or ushers should be notified and adequately instructed for their participation in serving the congregation. A diagram of the seating arrangement of the deacons and their positions in serving the congregation may be mimeographed and distributed.

Suggested Procedure

1. At the appropriate time in the order of worship, usually following the meditation (sermon), the pastor will take his stand back of the Lord's Supper table. The chairman of deacons and vice-chairman will then take their positions at each end of the table. If a linen is used to cover the elements, the chairman and vice-chairman will remove the cloth and fold it carefully. In most churches the covering is not deemed necessary.

2. The pastor may quote an appropriate passage of Scripture, such as 1 Corinthians 11:23–24.

"For I received from the Lord what I also delivered to you, that the Lord Jesus on the night when he was betrayed took bread, and when he had given thanks, he broke it, and said, 'This is my body which is for you. Do this in remembrance of me' " (RSV).

The pastor may then break a portion of the bread, or not, as he chooses.

3. The pastor will lead a prayer or call upon someone to lead a prayer such as:

"O Lord, we praise thee for the gift of thy Son Christ Jesus who died upon the cross. We do not presume to come to thy table trusting in our own righteousness, but in thy mercy. Forgive our transgressions, cleanse our hearts, and put a new spirit within us. Make us aware of the presence of our living Lord, in whose name we pray. Amen."

4. The deacons will stand as directed by the chairman and receive the bread plates from the chairman and vice-chairman. From this point appropriate organ music may be played while the deacons serve the congregation.

5. The deacons will proceed to their stations as previously assigned and serve the congregation.

6. When the congregation has been served, the deacons will return to the front of the sanctuary. The chairman and vice-chairman will take the plates and return them to the table.

7. The deacons will be seated. They will be served by the chairman (and the vice-chairman if the number is large).

8. The chairman and vice-chairman will return to

the table. The chairman of deacons will serve the pastor. The chairman and vice-chairman will serve themselves. (This procedure is subject to some variation, depending on the pastor's judgment. But he should agree with the deacons beforehand as to the procedure to be used.)

9. The pastor may quote an appropriate Scripture passage, such as Romans 12:1:

"I appeal to you therefore, brethren, by the mercies of God, to present your bodies as a living sacrifice, holy and acceptable to God, which is your spiritual worship" (RSV).

Then the pastor may lead the congregation in partaking of the broken bread.

10. The pastor may then quote 1 Corinthians 11: 25–26:

"In the same way also the cup, after supper, saying, 'This cup is the new covenant in my blood. Do this, as often as you drink it, in remembrance of me.' For as often as you eat this bread and drink the cup, you proclaim the Lord's death until he comes" (RSV).

After an appropriate prayer the deacons will proceed in serving the cup as they did in serving the bread.

11. The pastor may quote a passage of Scripture, then lead the congregation in partaking of the cup. If there are no containers in the pews for the cups, the deacons may collect the cups.

12. The congregation may sing a stanza of a closing hymn, such as:

My Jesus, I love Thee, I know Thou art mine;
For Thee all the follies of sin I resign;
My gracious Redeemer, my Saviour art Thou,
If ever I loved Thee, my Jesus, 'tis now.

Other appropriate hymns of dedication and commit-
ment which may be sung here are these: "Jesus Paid It
All"; "I Surrender All"; "Jesus, I My Cross Have Tak-
en"; "O for a Closer Walk with God"; "O Master, Let
Me Walk with Thee"; "Jesus, the Very Thought of
Thee"; "More Love to Thee, O Christ"; and others.

Scripture passages which may be used prior to the
administration of the Lord's Supper include:

Matthew 5:3-12	1 Corinthians 11:23-26
Matthew 5:13-16	1 Corinthians 12:27-31
Matthew 26:26-28	1 Corinthians 13:1-13
Mark 14:22-26	Ephesians 3:20 to 4:6
Luke 22:19-22	Ephesians 6:10-18
John 6:35-40	Philippians 2:1-11
John 6:53-58	Philippians 3:7-11
John 14:15-21	Philippians 3:12-16
John 17:1-10	Philippians 4:8-9
Romans 8:28-30	Colossians 3:15-17
Romans 8:35,37-39	Hebrews 11:1-3; 12:1-2
Romans 12:1-3	1 Peter 1:3-9
Romans 12:9-13	1 Peter 5:6-11
	Revelation 22:14,17,20-21

Part III

The Wedding

Marriage is one of life's primary experiences. The Christian wedding is a historic ceremony of dedication administered by the church and a ritual of commitment for those entering into marriage. In it God's blessings are invoked by the minister and the congregation. It is a celebration of God's establishment of the home as the primary social institution. The planning and performance of the wedding ceremony should therefore be carried out with seriousness, dignity, and joy.

Guiding Principles

1. Since a wedding involves many persons, the church should provide a wholesome atmosphere and a complete program of education in which youth may rightly mature in the matters of dating, becoming engaged, and planning for establishing Christian homes.

2. Prior to the wedding the minister should counsel the couple concerning such matters as the basic responsibility of commitment in a maturing relationship, vocation and home finances, mutual fulfilment in sexual relationships, planning for children, and the relation of the home to the church. The planning of the wedding as to the kind (formal or informal) and time and place (church or home), and procedures for the rehearsal and

the wedding ceremony should be agreed upon. The minister should make certain the couple understands the requirements of the law regarding marriage. The pastor may wish to give them a copy of a good book on marriage, such as Woods's *Harmony in Marriage* or David Mace's *Success in Marriage*.

3. Laws governing marriage and divorce are under the authority of the state and vary from state to state. The minister should familiarize himself with the laws of his state. A proper marriage license is uniformly required. Some states require a waiting period after the license is acquired. Blood tests (Wassermann or its equivalent) are required in most states. Some states require a minister to be ordained and to register with the court clerk. Immediately following the wedding the minister should fill in the marriage license, sign it, and promptly mail it personally to the office which issued it. He may provide the couple with a certificate of marraige. (For further detailed information see *The Cokesbury Marriage Manual*.)

4. Appropriate music should be chosen. Ordinary popular music should be avoided. Good hymns are often used today and may be sung by the congregation.

Processionals (hymns may be sung by congregation)

"For the Beauty of the Earth"
"God of Our Fathers, Whose Almighty Hand"
"Praise, My Soul, the King of Heaven"
"Praise the Lord! Ye Heavens, Adore Him"
"Praise to God, Immortal Praise"
"Praise to the Lord, the Almighty"

"We, Thy People, Praise Thee"
"Bride's Chorus" from *Lohengrin* by Wagner

Recessionals (hymns may be sung by congregation)

"Joyful, Joyful, We Adore Thee"
"Love Divine, All Loves Excelling"
"Now Thank We All Our God"
"O Master, Let Me Walk with Thee"
"Wedding March" by Mendelssohn

Wedding Hymns (may be used as an organ or vocal selection)

"Lord, Who at Cana's Wedding Feast"
"May the Grace of Christ Our Saviour"
"O Father, All Creating"
"O Love Divine and Golden"
"O Perfect Love"
"The King of Love My Shepherd Is"

Organ Music

"Arioso in A Major"; "Jesu, Joy of Man's Desiring";
    "Sheep May Safely Graze"; "Sinfonia" from *Wedding Cantata* (Bach)
"Cantabile" (Franck)

Slow Movements from Violin Concertos (Handel; Arr., Klein)

"Love Dream" (Liszt)
"Aria" (Peters)
"Serenade" (Schubert)
"Carillon" (Sowerby)

"Prelude on 'Rhosymedre' " (Vaughan Williams)
"Marriage at Cana in Galilee" (Weinberger)

Vocal Music

"Be Thou But Near"; "Jesus Shepherd, Be Near Me";
  "My Heart Ever Faithful"; "O Love That Casts
  Out Fear" (Bach)
"I Love You Truly" (Bond)
"Though I Speak with Tongues" (Brahms)
"O Perfect Love" (Burleigh)
"True Love Is God's Gift" (Chambers)
"Because" (d'Hardelot)
"A Wedding Prayer" (Dunlap)
"The Twenty-third Psalm"; "I Will Sing New Songs
  of Gladness" (Dvorak)
"O Lord Most Holy" (Franck)
"The Song of Ruth" (Gounod)
"Wedding Hymn" (Handel)
"A Wedding Benediction"; "We Lift Our Hearts to
  Thee" (Lovelace)
"Eternal Love" (Willan)

5. Etiquette is important in weddings. For example,
the minister should dress in keeping with that of the
wedding party. For the informal wedding an ordinary
street suit of dark blue, dark gray, or black, with black
shoes, white shirt, and dark accessories is appropriate.
For the formal wedding, if the party wears tuxedos, the
minister may wear a tuxedo or a cut-away dark gray
morning coat and vest, with gray and black striped
trousers, white shirt with turned-down collar and black

or black and gray ascot tie. If the wedding party wears full-dress (tails, standing or wing collar, white shirt with studs, white bow tie and white gloves), the minister may wear the same, or he may wear a robe.

6. Printed instructions, adopted by the church, concerning the use of church facilities may be given to those planning for weddings.

7. There should be no taking of flash pictures during the processional, the ceremony, or the recessional. They may be taken afterwards, before or during the reception.

The Rehearsal

1. The wedding rehearsal is usually held on the evening of the day before the wedding. Plans should be agreed upon ahead of time, especially the time for the rehearsal.

2. The minister should direct the rehearsal or designate someone else who knows the requirements of the church and the details of the processional, the ceremony, and the recessional.

3. All members of the wedding party, including the organist and soloist, should be present and on time at the rehearsal. Thorough drilling on the processional, the ceremony, and the recessional is essential if mistakes are to be avoided. An hour is sufficient for a formal wedding rehearsal. See the diagram on page 29 for a suggested order.

The Formal Wedding at the Church
The Processional

1. The wedding party should arrive twenty to thirty

minutes prior to the time for the ceremony. The organist may begin playing fifteen to twenty minutes early.

2. The groom's mother is seated by an usher in the first pew at the right facing the chancel. The groom's father will follow the usher and take his seat beside her.

3. The head usher will seat the bride's mother in the first pew at the left.

4. Candlelighters may then light the candles, or they may light the candles earlier as organ music is played.

5. The soloist and/or the choir may sing.

6. The processional will now begin. The processional may be played by the organist or a processional hymn may be sung by the congregation.

7. The minister will enter from the right side of the chancel, when building arrangements permit, followed by the groom and the groomsman. Others will enter from the rear of the sanctuary and take their places. See the diagram below.

8. The ushers will march down the center aisle (or the left aisle) two by two, in order of height, the shortest first. The number of ushers and bridesmaids may vary.

9. Bridesmaids will enter singly and take their positions in front of the ushers in order of height. Or, all the ushers may take their positions on the groom's side of the altar and all the bridesmaids on the bride's side of the altar.

10. The maid of honor will enter followed by the flower girl and the ring bearer (if any).

11. The bride and her father (or whoever gives her) will enter, he walking on her left. When they approach

the altar, she will release her father's arm. The groom
will take her right hand and draw it through the bend
of his left arm. When the minister asks, "Who gives the
bride to be married?" the father will answer, "I do" or
"Her mother and I," and take his seat in the pew beside
his wife.

12. The bride and groom and the maid of honor and
groomsman will step forward near the minister. The
entire wedding party, which has stood facing the audi-
ence, may now face the minister.

The diagram on page 29 suggests six ushers and six
bridesmaids. There may be fewer or more according to
the wishes of the bride.

When a Minister's Daughter Marries

When a minister's daughter marries, he may officiate
and also give the daughter in marriage.

A fellow minister may be asked to assist in the wedding. He will begin the service and proceed through the
question, "Who gives the bride in marriage?" The father
of the bride, having presented her to the assisting minister, will take his place beside the other minister and
assume the part of the officiating minister, asking the
questions and making the pronouncement of marriage.

Suggested Formal Ceremony

In many churches the marriage ceremony is written
by the individual minister. However, he may wish to
follow a traditional ceremony such as that of the Epis-
copal church. If he does, it will be more meaningful if
he will use contemporary language in the ceremony.

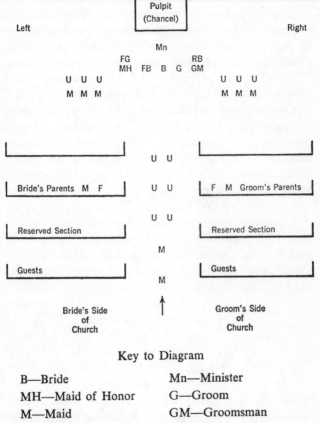

Key to Diagram

B—Bride	Mn—Minister
MH—Maid of Honor	G—Groom
M—Maid	GM—Groomsman
FG—Flower Girl	U—Usher
MB—Mother of Bride	RB—Ring Bearer
FB—Father of Bride	MG—Mother of Groom
	FG—Father of Groom

Certain general elements should be included, such as
(1) the purpose of the gathering, (2) the meaning of
marriage, (3) the charge to the couple, (4) questions
to the bride and groom, (5) the affirming of commitments, (6) the pronouncement of the marriage, and
(7) a prayer of petition and dedication asking God's
blessings upon the newly established home.

The following ceremony for a formal wedding may
serve as a guide for the minister who constructs his own
ceremony, or it may be used as it is if he desires. Certain
parts of the ceremony, such as repeating the phrase
"With this ring I pledge" and so forth, may be omitted.
Some couples prefer a briefer ceremony. The minister
will use his own discretion as to the length, as long as
it is reasonably brief and the essential elements are included. The ceremony may be read or it may be repeated from memory. The entire ceremony, including
the processional and the recessional, usually takes ten
to twenty minutes.

MINISTER: Dear friends [or dearly beloved, or
beloved friends], we are here assembled in the
presence of God to unite A——[groom's name]
and B——[bride's name] in marriage.

The Bible teaches that marriage is to be a permanent relationship of one man and one woman
freely and totally committed to each other as companions for life. Our Lord declared that man shall
leave his father and mother and unite with his wife

in the building of a home, and the two shall become one flesh.

Who gives the bride to be married?

BRIDE'S FATHER: I do [*or he may say, "Her mother and I"*].   Lou's SONG

MINISTER: The home is built upon love, which virtue is best portrayed in the thirteenth chapter of Paul's first letter to the Corinthians. "Love is patient and kind; love is not jealous or boastful; it is not arrogant or rude. Love does not insist on its own way; it is not irritable or resentful; it does not rejoice at wrong, but rejoices in the right. Love bears all things, believes all things, hopes all things, endures all things. Love never ends; . . . So faith, hope, love abide, these three; but the greatest of these is love" [*1 Cor. 13:4–13,RSV*].

Marriage is a companionship which involves mutual commitment and responsibility. You will share alike in the responsibilites and the joys of life. When companions share a sorrow the sorrow is halved, and when they share a joy the joy is doubled.

You are exhorted to dedicate your home to your Creator. Take his Word, the Bible, for your guide. Give loyal devotion to his church, thus uniting the mutual strength of these two most important institutions, living your lives as his willing servants, and

true happiness will be your temporal and eternal
reward.

Let us pray. O Lord of life and love, bestow thy
grace upon this marriage, and seal this commitment
of thy children with thy love.

As thou hast brought them together by thy divine
providence, sanctify them by thy Spirit, that they
may give themselves fully one to the other and to
thee. Give them strength and patience to live their
lives in a manner that will mutually bless themselves and honor thy holy name, through Jesus
Christ our Lord. Amen.

*(The minister will ask them to join their right hands
and take the following vows):*

MINISTER TO GROOM: A——, will you take
B——to be your wife; will you commit yourself
to her happiness and her self-fulfilment as a person,
and to her usefulness in God's kingdom; and will
you promise to love, honor, trust, and serve her in
sickness and in health, in adversity and prosperity,
and to be true and loyal to her, so long as you both
shall live?

GROOM: I will.

MINISTER TO BRIDE: B——, will you take
A——to be your husband; will you commit yourself to his happiness and his self-fulfilment as a
person, and to his usefulness in God's kingdom;

and do you promise to love, honor, trust, and serve
him in sickness and in health, in adversity and
prosperity, and to be true and loyal to him, so long
as you both shall live?

BRIDE: I will.

*(If the wedding ring is to be used, the bride will hand
her bouquet to the maid of honor when the ceremony
starts. The engagement ring will be left at home or trans-
ferred to the right hand prior to the processional. The
minister will receive the ring from the groomsman and
proceed.)*

MINISTER: The wedding ring is a symbol of
marriage in at least two ways: the purity of gold
symbolizes the purity of your love for each other,
and the unending circle symbolizes the unending
vows which you are taking, which may be broken
honorably in the sight of God only by death. As a
token of your vows, you will give and receive the
ring [*or rings*].

MINISTER TO GROOM: A——, *LAWRENCE* you will give the
ring and repeat after me: "B——, *LAURIE* with this ring I
pledge my life and love to you, in the name of the
Father, and of the Son, and of the Holy Spirit."
[*The Groom repeats this.*]

MINISTER TO BRIDE: B—— *LAURIE*, you will give the
ring and repeat after me: "A——, *LAWRENCE* with this ring I
pledge my love and life to you, in the name of the

Father, and of the Son, and of the Holy Spirit."
[*The Bride repeats this.*]

(*In the case of a single ring ceremony, the bride will
say, "A——, I accept this ring and pledge to you my love
and life, in the name of the Father, and of the Son, and of
the Holy Spirit."*)

MINISTER: Will both of you please repeat after
me:

> Entreat me not to leave you
> or to return from following you;
> for where you go I will go,
> and where you lodge I will lodge;
> your people shall be my people,
> and your God my God [*Ruth 1:16,RSV*].

[*The Couple repeats this.*]

MINISTER TO CONGREGATION: Since they have
made these commitments before God and this assembly [*or, these witnesses*], by the authority of
God and the laws of this state, I declare that
A_____ and B_____ are husband and wife.

MINISTER TO COUPLE: A_____ and B_____, you
are no longer two independent persons but one.
"What therefore God has joined together, let no
man separate" [*Matt. 19:6, NASB**].

(*The bride and groom may now kneel, and the minister*

---

* *New American Standard Bible, New Testament.* © The
Lockman Foundation, 1960, 1962, 1963.

*may express a free prayer. Or the Model Prayer (Matt.
6:9-14, KJV) may be repeated by the minister and the
bride and groom, or by the entire congregation.)*

Our Father which art in heaven, Hallowed be thy
name.
Thy kingdom come. Thy will be done in earth,
as it is in heaven.
Give us this day our daily bread.
And forgive us our debts, as we forgive our
debtors.
And lead us not into temptation, but deliver us
from evil:
For thine is the kingdom, and the power, and
the glory, for ever. Amen.

*(The minister may then add the benediction; it may
either be one of his own composition or a passage of
Scripture, such as one of those given below.)*

The Lord bless you and keep you:
The Lord make his face to shine upon you, and
be gracious to you:
The Lord lift up his countenance upon you, and
give you peace [*Num. 6:24–26,RSV*].

The grace of the Lord Jesus Christ and the love
of God and the fellowship of the Holy Spirit be
with you all [*2 Cor. 13:14,RSV*]. Amen.

The Recessional

1. Following the ceremony, the groom may or may not kiss the bride. The bride will then take her bouquet from the maid of honor, turn toward her husband, and place her left hand through his right arm. The recessional will begin immediately, and the wedding party will walk briskly down the center aisle (or down the right aisle facing the altar, if there is no center aisle) in the following order: (1) bride and groom, (2) flower girl and ring bearer, (3) groomsman and matron or maid of honor, (4) ushers and bridesmaids by pairs.

2. The head usher will escort the bride's mother from the church, the father following behind.

3. Another usher will escort the groom's mother from the church, the father following behind.

4. The minister will retire at the place where he entered, this being the signal for the congregation to disassemble.

The Reception

The wedding reception may be held at the church, the home, or some other place such as a social club. At a reception the bride and groom may receive. Or, the following may stand in this order in the reception line: the mother of the bride, the father of the groom, the mother of the groom, the father of the bride, the bride, the groom, the maid (or matron) of honor, and the bridesmaids.

The minister should show a courtesy by attending the reception even when it may differ from his own tastes. Having greeted the wedding party he should then retire into the background, remembering that the party belongs to the bride and groom. He may or may not stay until the reception is concluded, but before he leaves, he should pay his respects to the parents of the bride and then gracefully retire.

The guests will be served refreshments according to plan. The bride then retires to the room assigned her to dress for going away. The groom also goes to the room assigned him and dresses for going away. Then they return to express their appreciation to family and friends and to receive good wishes as they depart. The bride may toss her bouquet to the bridesmaids as she leaves to dress, or as she is leaving the church.

The bride's parents are responsible for the cost of florist's decorations, the reception, the organist's fee (if any) and soloist's fee (if any), the building fee (if any) and the caretaker's fee. The groom is responsible for the minister's honorarium, flowers for the bride and the two mothers, and the planning and cost of the honeymoon.

The Informal Wedding

The bride and her family may prefer an informal wedding in their home, in the home of the minister, in the church chapel, or in the minister's study. The couple may wish to be accompanied by their parents only or by a few friends.

The informal wedding ceremony is usually somewhat briefer than the formal ceremony. It includes all of the essentials of a ceremony, particularly the taking of vows and the pronouncement of the marriage. Certain lines ordinarily repeated after the minister may be omitted. In any case, the ceremony should be conducted reverently and with dignity.

Suggested Informal Ceremony

The following brief ceremony may be used in the informal wedding. The wedding party will assemble informally. The minister will take his stand and indicate where the bride and groom will stand, and their attendants also, if there are any. The ceremony will then proceed.

MINISTER: Friends, we are assembled here to unite A——— and B——— in marriage. The Bible teaches that marriage is of divine origin. The home is God's gift to man.

Marriage is a commitment which one man and one woman make to each other and to God. The vows you are about to make should be kept seriously as long as you both live.

MINISTER TO COUPLE: A——— and B———, you will now join your right hands together and make the following vows.

MINISTER TO GROOM: A———, will you take B——— to be your lawful wife, and will you promise to love, honor, and support her, keeping only to her, as long as you both live?

GROOM: I will.

MINISTER TO BRIDE: B———, will you take

A_____ to be your lawful husband, and will you promise to love, honor, and cooperate with him, keeping only to him, as long as you both live?

BRIDE: I will.

MINISTER: Since you have made these vows, by the authority of the state and as a minister of the gospel of Jesus Christ, I now pronounce that you are husband and wife. Whom God has joined together, let not man separate.

(Prayer for God's blessings upon the marriage.)

The minister will congratulate the couple. If there is to be no reception, the family and friends will also offer their congratulations at this time.

Note: For further instructions see Amy Vanderbilt, *Etiquette;* Emily Post, *Etiquette;* Mrs. Burton Kingsland, *The Book of Weddings;* May Detherage, *Planning Your Wedding;* Elizabeth Swadley, *Your Christian Wedding.*

The Home Wedding

When the wedding is held in the home of the bride, the plan suggested for the formal wedding at the church may be used, with certain necessary adjustments. The bride's mother will stand at the door and greet the guests, and the groom's parents will be seated with other friends.

An improvised altar may be constructed inside the home or on the lawn. The minister, groom, and the best man enter through one door and the bridal party through another. If there is a stairway the bridal party usually enters from there. A processional may be played. There is no recessional. Following the benediction, the minister should extend his best wishes for their happiness and congratulate the groom. Friends may then gather about them to offer their congratulations.

The Renewal of Vows

A service for renewal of vows may be requested by married couples at wedding anniversaries or upon other significant occasions. This is particularly fitting for the golden wedding anniversary conducted in the home. A renewal service may also be conducted at a regular worship service when all married couples will renew their vows as an emphasis upon the Christian home.

The minister may read an appropriate passage of Scripture, emphasizing the importance of the home. He then may use the following ceremony.

MINISTER: Friends, we are here assembled in the presence of God to witness the renewal of the marriage vows taken by this couple, A_____ and B_____ [or, these couples], when they were united in holy marriage. God is always pleased when we rededicate our lives and our homes by an act of worship.

(The minister may add any other thoughts appropriate to the particular situation.)

MINISTER: You will now please unite your right hands.

Do you now promise to renew the vows which you made when you were first united in marriage?

COUPLE [*or couples*]: We do.

MINISTER: Do you promise to continue to keep the vows and the covenant which you made at your wedding?

COUPLE: We do.

MINISTER: Do you promise to continue to cultivate your love for each other by discipline, understanding, trustfulness, compassion, thoughtfulness, patience, and mutual consideration?

COUPLE: We do.

MINISTER: Do you promise to endeavor to create a Christian environment in your home and to help each other to live godly lives in Christian service?

COUPLE: We do.

MINISTER: Because of the vows which you have renewed with each other and with God in the presence of these witnesses, let us now join in a prayer of dedication.

(*The minister will now pray for the couple or couples, for the home, for the church, and for the kingdom of God.*)

Following the prayer, a hymn of thanksgiving and praise to God may be sung by the company present. The entire order of service may be planned with creative imagination for the good of all concerned.

Part IV

The Funeral Service

The Christian funeral is a service provided by the church to give comfort and guidance to persons suffering from grief. Helpful ceremonial procedures may aid them in working through their grief and in finding wholeness of being and purpose for future living. The primary purpose of the funeral service is to exalt the meaning of life and to encourage persons in grief to adjust to God's claim upon their lives.

The funeral service is an act in which the church shows its concern for those who suffer loss. The congregation offers its fellowship in an effort to strengthen its people in the crisis of death. English statesman William Gladstone said, "Show me the manner in which a nation or a community cares for its dead, and I will measure with mathematical exactness the character of its people, their respect for the laws of the land, and their loyalty to high ideals."

The funeral is also an appropriate memorial for the person who has died. Christianity considers the dignity of man in life and also in death.

Guiding Principles

1. Immediately upon hearing of the death of a person, the minister should go immediately to the family,

whether in the hospital or in the home. A few quiet words, a Scripture verse, and a brief prayer are usually offered. If asked to conduct the funeral service, he will arrange to come later to assist in making the plans.

2. At the appointed time the minister will go to the home to plan for the funeral service. The time for the funeral should be decided by the family, the funeral director, and the pastor. The minister will try to meet the requests of the family for music and other items in the service, so long as they are in good taste and in keeping with the Christian content and order.

3. The primary purpose of the funeral service is to aid people in working through their grief in a normal fashion. The minister should not seek to stir the emotions but should encourage grieving persons to express their emotions normally.

4. The funeral service should lead people to face the reality of death as well as the reality of life.

5. In this worship service the church has an opportunity through the minister to express its affirmation of Christian faith. The great truths of Christianity, especially the power of the resurrection and the meaning of Christian commitment, should be set forth.

6. A brief funeral meditation is usually appropriate. Its purpose should be to interpret, to affirm truth, to support and comfort the bereaved, and to provide a challenge for future living. The minister should neither condemn nor stress the faults and sins of the dead. The truth of God's Word will provide the necessary interpretation.

7. Viewing the body can be meaningful in accept-

ing the reality of death and separation and loss. This should be done prior to the service. The casket should probably be closed at the service to indicate the place of separation and to point to the spiritual and eternal values.

8. A personal eulogy, when appropriate, may be used. Extravagant praise should usually be avoided. A eulogy is not absolutely essential. There are times when it is better to say little or nothing about the deceased.

9. A funeral service is not the end of the church's ministry. The minister and other friends should visit in the home as often and as long as necessary to provide support and guidance. The bereaved person often goes through a period of shock. He is better able a little later to receive the help offered by the minister.

10. The church and community should be encouraged to remember the bereaved in prayer and to minister to them, helping them to adjust to life and to relate to meaningful groups.

Order of Service

The minister will usually arrange the order of service appropriate to the particular situation. This may call for many variations. The following order is one which has been used often by ministers.

PRELUDE MUSIC
PROCESSIONAL

The minister always precedes the casket unless it has already been placed prior to the time of the service. The congregation will stand as the minister enters. The minister will take his place in the pulpit and stand until the family is seated.

A HYMN

This may be sung by congregation, choir, quartet, or soloist, or it may be played by the organ if no vocal music is used.

SCRIPTURE READING

Lord, thou hast been our dwelling place in all generations. Before the mountains were brought forth, or ever thou hadst formed the earth and the world, even from everlasting to everlasting, thou art God. . . . For a thousand years in thy sight are but as yesterday when it is past, and as a watch in the night. . . . So teach us to number our days, that we may apply our hearts unto wisdom. . . . O satisfy us early with thy mercy; that we may rejoice and be glad all our days. . . Let thy work appear unto thy servants, and thy glory unto their children. And let the beauty of the Lord our God be upon us: and establish thou the work of our hands upon us; yea, the work of our hands establish thou it [*Psalm 90,KJV*].

Draw nigh to God, and he will draw nigh to you. Cleanse your hands, ye sinners; and purify your hearts, ye double-minded. . . . humble yourselves in the sight of the Lord, and he shall lift you up [*James 4:8–10,KJV*].

PRAYER

Almighty God, thou who dost give life to man and dost receive him again in death, we thank thee for thy abiding presence and for the grace provided in Christ Jesus. In our frailty we look to thee for strength and in our sorrow for comfort. Help us in this hour to put our trust in thee that we may receive light and understanding and a new experience of thy grace unto eternal hope, through Jesus Christ our Lord. Amen.

A HYMN

This may be sung by congregation, choir, quartet, or soloist, or played by the organ only.

SCRIPTURE READING

The Lord is my shepherd; I shall not want. He maketh me to lie down in green pastures: he leadeth me beside the still waters. He restoreth my soul: he leadeth me in the paths of righteousness for his name's sake. Yea, though I walk through the valley of the shadow of death, I will fear no evil: for thou art with me; thy rod and thy staff they comfort me. Thou preparest a table before me in the presence of mine enemies: thou anointest my head with oil; my cup runneth over. Surely goodness and mercy shall follow me all the days of my life: and I will dwell in the house of the Lord for ever [*Psalm 23,KJV*].

Let not your heart be troubled: ye believe in God, believe also in me. In my Father's house are many mansions: if it were not so, I would have told you. I go to prepare a place for you. And if I go and prepare a place for you, I will come again, and receive you unto myself; that where I am, there ye may be also. . . . I will not leave you comfortless: I will come to you. Yet a little while, and the world seeth me no more; but ye see me: because I live, ye shall live also. . . . Peace I leave with you, my peace I give unto you: not as the world giveth, give I unto you. Let not your heart be troubled, neither let it be afraid [*John 14:1–27,KJV*].

Who shall separate us from the love of Christ? Shall tribulation, or distress, or persecution, or famine, or nakedness, or peril, or sword? As it is written, For thy sake we are killed all the day long; we are accounted as sheep for the slaughter. Nay, in all these things we are more than conquerors through him that loved us. For I am persuaded, that neither death, nor life, nor angels, nor principalities, nor powers, nor things present, nor things to come, nor height, nor depth, nor any other creature, shall be able to separate us from the love of God, which is in Christ Jesus our Lord [*Rom. 8:35–39,KJV*].

But we would not have you ignorant, brethren, concerning those who are asleep, that ye may not grieve as others do who have no hope. For since we believe that Jesus died and rose again, even so, through Jesus, God will bring with him those who have fallen asleep. For this we declare to you by the word of the Lord, that we who are alive, who are left until the coming of the Lord, shall not precede those who have fallen asleep. For the Lord himself will descend from heaven with a cry of command, with the archangel's call, and with the sound of the trumpet of God. And the dead in Christ will rise first; then we who are alive, who are left, shall be caught up together with them in the clouds to meet the Lord in the air; and so we shall always be with the Lord. Therefore comfort one another with these words [*1 Thess. 4:13–18,RSV*].

Truly, truly, I say to you, the hour is coming, and now is, when the dead will hear the voice of the Son of God, and those who hear will live. For as the Father has life in himself, so he has granted the Son also to have life in himself, and has given him authority to execute judgment, because he is the Son of man. Do not marvel at this; for the hour is coming when all who are in the tombs will hear his voice and come forth, those who have done good, to the resurrection of life, and those who have done evil, to the resurrection of judgment [*John 5:25–29,RSV*].

If in this life we who are in Christ have only hope, we are of all men most to be pitied. But in fact Christ has been raised from the dead, the first fruits of those who have fallen asleep. For as by a man came death, by a man has come also the resurrection of the dead. For as in Adam all die, so also in Christ shall all be made alive [*1 Cor. 15:19–22,RSV*].

Then I saw a new heaven and a new earth; for the first heaven and the first earth had passed away, and the sea was no more. And I saw the holy city, new Jerusalem, coming down out of heaven from God, prepared as a bride adorned for her husband; and I heard a great voice from the throne saying, 'Behold, the dwelling of God is with men. He will dwell with them, and they shall be his people, and God himself will be with them; he will wipe away every tear from their eyes, and death shall be no more, neither shall there be mourning nor crying nor pain any more, for the former things have passed away. . . . He who conquers shall have this heritage, and I will be his God and he shall be my son [*Rev. 21:1–7,RSV*].

PRAYER

Our gracious Father, we thank thee for the ties of love that bind thy children together and for the contributions which this thy servant has left among those who loved him [*her*].

Thou who art the God of comfort, look with compassion upon these who are bereaved, whose hearts are bowed down with grief. Give them understanding hearts that they may welcome thy grace and comfort. May this occasion be one of recommitment to thee, for thou art concerned about life in the present and in the future as well as in the past. May the fellowship of the church strengthen and support these who mourn and bring assurance of thy love to them in the name of Christ our Lord. Amen.

A HYMN

This may be sung by congregation, choir, quartet, or soloist, or played by the organ only.

MESSAGE

The obituary is usually read at this time. A brief

meditation (six to ten minutes) appropriate to the occasion may be given. A eulogy may be included or
omitted as desired.

BENEDICTION

Now to him who is able to keep you from falling
and to present you without blemish before the
presence of his glory with rejoicing, to the only
God, our Savior through Jesus Christ our Lord, be
glory, majesty, dominion, and authority, before all
time and now and for ever. Amen [*Jude 24–25,
RSV*].

The Graveside Service

At the cemetery the minister will precede the casket
from the hearse to the grave. The funeral director may
walk with him.

The casket having been placed and the flowers arranged under the supervision of the funeral director, the
minister will take his stand at the head of the casket.

SCRIPTURE

Fear not, I am the first and the last, and the
living one; I died, and behold I am alive for evermore [*Rev. 1:17–18,RSV*].

Because I live, ye shall live also [*John 14:19,
KJV*].

Blessed are the dead who die in the Lord henceforth . . . that they may rest from their labors, for
their deeds follow them! [*Rev. 14:13,RSV*].

Lo! I tell you a mystery. We shall not all sleep, but we shall all be changed, in a moment, in the twinkling of an eye, at the last trumpet. For the trumpet will sound, and the dead will be raised imperishable, and we shall be changed. For this perishable nature must put on the imperishable, and this mortal nature must put on immortality. When the perishable puts on the imperishable, and the mortal puts on immortality, then shall come to pass the saying that is written: "Death is swallowed up in victory. O Death, where is thy victory? O death, where is thy sting?" . . . thanks be to God, who gives us the victory through our Lord Jesus Christ [*1 Cor. 15:51–57,RSV*].

Let not your heart be troubled: ye believe in God, believe also in me. In my Father's house are many mansions: if it were not so, I would have told you. I go to prepare a place for you. And if I go and prepare a place for you, I will come again, and receive you unto myself; that where I am, there ye may be also [*John 14:1–3,KJV*].

PRAYER

O Lord of life and death, we acknowledge the reality of death. Although it separates loved ones, make us aware that it is only for a season. Although it brings grief, may we look to thy spirit to bring comfort and peace to these who mourn. Although it brings disappointment, give us faith to look to the future with hope and confidence and courage. Now, O Father, abide with these our friends throughout the coming days, and bring us all together again around thy throne in eternal glory. This we pray in the name of Jesus Christ our living Lord. Amen.

The minister may now speak a parting word to the family and indicate to them that he will visit with them again in their home. He may then proceed to his car.

The Memorial Service

A memorial service is often held in memory of a person, even though the body may have been interred earlier, lost at sea, buried abroad, and so on. The service should follow an order similar to that of a regular funeral service. At least, it should center on the worship of God. An appropriate meditation should be carefully planned by the minister.

The Joint Service

When other ministers are invited to assist in a funeral service, the pastor of the deceased at whose church the service is held usually takes charge and conducts the service. He will outline the service and indicate the parts which the other ministers will take, the Scripture readings, the prayers, and so forth. He will usually have the meditation and the eulogy, unless the family has requested some other minister to have this part. He may introduce the other participating ministers, or they may simply rise for the assigned order.

When other organizations participate, such as the Armed Forces or some fraternal order like the Masons, details should be carefully worked out and agreed upon prior to the service. These organizations usually assist at the graveside service only. The minister in charge usually has the closing sentences and the benediction.

Suggested Further Resources

The following Scripture passages, themes, hymns, and poems may be found helpful in planning funeral services. The minister may at times desire to read appropriate hymns and poems as a part of his funeral sermon.

For the Elderly

For we know that if the earthly tent we live in is destroyed, we have a building from God, a house not made with hands, eternal in the heavens. Here indeed we groan, and long to put on our heavenly dwelling, so that by putting it on we may not be found naked. For while we are still in this tent, we sigh with anxiety; not that we would be unclothed, but that we would be further clothed, so that what is mortal may be swallowed up by life. He who has prepared us for this very thing is God, who has given us the Spirit as a guarantee. So we are always

of good courage; we know that while we are at
home in the body we are away from the Lord, for
we walk by faith, not by sight. We are of good
courage, and we would rather be away from the
body and at home with the Lord. So whether we
are at home or away, we make it our aim to please
him. For we must all appear before the judgment
seat of Christ, so that each one may receive good
or evil, according to what he has done in the body
[2 Cor. 5:1–10,RSV].

So we do not lose heart. Though our outer nature
is wasting away, our inner nature is being renewed
every day. For this slight momentary affliction is
preparing for us an eternal weight of glory beyond
all comparison, because we look not to the things
that are seen but to the things that are unseen; for
the things that are seen are transient, but the things
that are unseen are eternal [2 Cor. 4:16–18,RSV].

For as many as are led by the Spirit of God,
they are the sons of God. For ye have not received
the spirit of bondage again to fear; but ye have
received the Spirit of adoption, whereby we cry,
Abba, Father. The Spirit itself beareth witness with
our spirit, that we are the children of God: And if
children, then heirs; heirs of God, and joint-heirs
with Christ, if so be that we suffer with him, that

we may be also glorified together. For I reckon that
the sufferings of this present time are not worthy
to be compared with the glory which shall be revealed in us. . . . And we know that all things
work together for good to them that love God,
to them who are the called according to his purpose. For whom he did foreknow, he also did predestinate to be conformed to the image of his Son,
that he might be the firstborn among many brethren. Moreover, whom he did predestinate, them he
also called: and whom he called, them he also justified: and whom he justified, them he also glorified [*Rom. 8:14–30,KJV*].

For I am now ready to be offered, and the time
of my departure is at hand. I have fought a good
fight, I have finished my course, I have kept the
faith: Henceforth there is laid up for me a crown
of righteousness, which the Lord, the righteous
judge, shall give me at that day: and not to me
only, but unto all them also that love his appearing
[*2 Tim. 4:6–8,KJV*]

For a Woman

Who can find a virtuous woman? for her price
is far above rubies. The heart of her husband doth
safely trust in her, so that he shall have no need of

spoil. She will do him good and not evil all the days
of her life. . . . She stretcheth out her hand to
the poor; yea, she reacheth forth her hands to the
needy. She is not afraid of the snow for her household: for all her household are clothed with scarlet.
. . . Strength and honor are her clothing; and she
shall rejoice in time to come. She openeth her mouth
with wisdom; and in her tongue is the law of kindness. She looketh well to the ways of her household, and eateth not the bread of idleness. Her
children arise up, and call her blessed; her husband
also, and he praiseth her. Many daughters have
done virtuously, but thou excellest them all. Favour
is deceitful, and beauty is vain: but a woman that
feareth the Lord, she shall be praised. Give her of
the fruit of her hands; and let her own works
praise her in the gates [*Prov. 31:10–31,KJV*].

For Children and Youth

At that time the disciples came to Jesus, saying,
"Who is the greatest in the kingdom of heaven?"
And calling to him a child, he put him in the
midst of them, and said, "Truly, I say to you, unless you turn and become like children, you will
never enter the kingdom of heaven. Whoever
humbles himself like this child, he is the greatest
in the kingdom of heaven. Whoever receives one

such child in my name receives me; but whoever causes one of these little ones who believe in me to sin, it would be better for him to have a great millstone fastened round his neck and to be drowned in the depth of the sea" [*Matt. 18:1–6, RSV*].

And they were bringing children to him, that he might touch them; and the disciples rebuked them. But when Jesus saw it he was indignant, and said to them, "Let the children come to me, do not hinder them; for to such belongs the kingdom of God. Truly, I say to you, whoever does not receive the kingdom of God like a child shall not enter it." And he took them in his arms and blessed them, laying his hands upon them [*Mark 10:13–16, RSV*].

Rejoice, O young man, in your youth, and let your heart cheer you in the days of your youth; walk in the ways of your heart and the sight of your eyes. . . . Remember also your Creator in the days of your youth, before the evil days come, and the years draw nigh, when you will say, "I have no pleasure in them"; . . . The end of the matter; all has been heard. Fear God, and keep his commandments; for this is the whole duty of man. For God will bring every deed in to judgment, with every secret thing, whether good or evil [*Eccl. 11:9 to 12:14,RSV*].

David . . . besought God for the child; and David fasted, and went in and lay all night upon the ground. . . . [*2 Sam. 12,RSV*].

Other Suggested Texts

The Lord is my light and my salvation; whom shall I fear? the Lord is the strength of my life; of whom shall I be afraid? . . . [*Psalm 27,KJV*].

"As the hart panteth after the water brooks, so panteth my soul after thee, O God. . . ." [*Psalm 42, KJV*].

Comfort, comfort my people, says your God. . . . He will feed his flock like a shepherd, he will gather the lambs in his arms, he will carry them in his bosom, and gently lead those that are with young. . . . The Lord is the everlasting God, the Creator of the ends of the earth. . . . They who wait for the Lord shall renew their strength, they shall mount up with wings like eagles, they shall run and not be weary, they shall walk and not faint [*Isa. 40:1–31,RSV*].

Man that is born of a woman is of few days, and full of trouble. . . . If a man die, shall he live again? All the days of my appointed time will I wait, till my change come [*Job 14:1–14,KJV*].

O Lord, thou hast searched me, and known me. . . . Search me, O God, and know my heart: try me, and know my thoughts: And see if there be any wicked way in me and lead me in the way everlasting [*Psalm 139:1–24,KJV*].

I will lift up mine eyes unto the hills, from whence cometh my help. . . . The Lord shall preserve thy going out and thy coming in from this time forth, and even for evermore [*Psalm 121, KJV*].

Blessed are the poor in spirit: for theirs is the kingdom of heaven [*Matt. 5:3–12, KJV*].

As a father pities his children, so the Lord pities those who fear him [*Psalm 103:13–22, RSV*].

I have fought the good fight, I have finished my course, I have kept the faith: Henceforth there is laid up for me a crown of righteousness, which the Lord, the righteous judge, shall give me at that day: and not to me only, but unto all them also that love his appearing [*2 Tim. 4:7–8, KJV*].

Well done, thou good and faithful servant [*Matt. 25:21, KJV*].

Jesus said to them, "I am the bread of life; he who comes to me shall not hunger, and he who believes in me shall never thirst. . . . For this is the will of my Father, that every one who sees the Son and believes in him should have eternal life; and I will raise him up at the last day" [*John 6:35–40, RSV*].

Now a certain man was ill, Lazarus of Bethany, the village of Mary and her sister Martha. . . . Now when Jesus came, he found that Lazarus had already been in the tomb four days. . . .

Jesus said to her, "I am the resurrection and the life; he who believes in me, though he die, yet shall he live, and whoever lives and believes in me shall never die" [*John 11:1–26, RSV*].

She was full of good works and acts of charity [*Acts 9:36, RSV*].

Finally, be strong in the Lord and in the strength of his might. Put on the whole armor of God, that you may be able to stand against the wiles of the devil. . . . [*Eph. 6:10–24, RSV*].

And I heard a voice from heaven saying, "Write this: Blessed are the dead who die in the Lord henceforth." "Blessed indeed," says the Spirit, "that

they may rest from their labors, for their deeds
follow them" [*Rev. 14:13, RSV*].

Appropriate Hymns (may be read or sung)

O Love That Wilt Not Let Me Go

O Love that wilt not let me go,
I rest my weary soul in thee;
I give thee back the life I owe,
That in thine ocean depths its flow
May richer, fuller be.

O Light that followest all my way,
I yield my flick'ring torch to thee;
My heart restores its borrowed ray,
That in thy sunshine's glow its day
May brighter, fairer be.

O Joy that seekest me through pain,
I cannot close my heart to thee;
I trace the rainbow through the rain,
And feel the promise is not vain
That morn shall tearless be.

O Cross that liftest up my head,
I dare not ask to hide from thee;
I lay in dust life's glory dead,
And from the ground there blossoms red
Life that shall endless be.

O God, Our Help in Ages Past

O God, our help in ages past,
Our hope for years to come,
Our shelter from the stormy blast,
And our eternal home!

Under the shadow of Thy throne
Thy saints have dwelt secure;
Sufficient is Thine arm alone,
And our defense is sure.

Before the hills in order stood,
Or earth received her frame,
From everlasting Thou art God,
To endless years the same.

A thousand ages in Thy sight
Are like an evening gone;
Short as the watch that ends the night
Before the rising sun.

O God, our help in ages past,
Our hope for years to come,
Be Thou our guard while life shall last,
And our eternal home.

Abide with Me

Abide with me: fast falls the eventide;
The darkness deepens; Lord, with me abide:

When other helpers fail, and comforts flee,
Help of the helpless, O abide with me!

Swift to its close ebbs out life's little day;
Earth's joys grow dim, its glories pass away:
Change and decay in all around I see:
O Thou who changest not, abide with me!

I need Thy presence every passing hour;
What but Thy grace can foil the tempter's power?
Who like Thyself my guide and stay can be?
Through cloud and sunshine, O abide with me!

Hold Thou Thy cross before my closing eyes;
Shine through the gloom, and point me to the skies:
Heaven's morning breaks and earth's vain shadows
    flee:
In life, in death, O Lord, abide with me!

There's a Wideness in God's Mercy

There's a wideness in God's mercy,
Like the wideness of the sea;
There's a kindness in His justice,
Which is more than liberty.

There is welcome for the sinner,
And more graces for the good;
There is mercy with the Saviour;
There is healing in His blood.

For the love of God is broader
Than the measure of man's mind;
And the heart of the Eternal
Is most wonderfully kind.

If our love were but more simple
We should take Him at His word;
And our lives would be all sunshine
In the sweetness of our Lord.

God Moves in a Mysterious Way

God moves in a mysterious way
His wonders to perform;
He plants His footsteps in the sea,
And rides upon the storm.

Ye fearful saints, fresh courage take;
The clouds ye so much dread
Are big with mercy, and shall break
With blessing on thy head.

Judge not the Lord by feeble sense,
But trust Him for His grace;
Behind a frowning providence
He hides a smiling face.

Blind unbelief is sure to err,
And scan His work in vain,
God is His own interpreter,
And He will make it plain.

Other Favorite Hymn Titles

"Come, Ye Disconsolate"

"Jesus, Saviour, Pilot Me"

"Lead, Kindly Light"

"My Faith Looks Up to Thee"

"My Jesus, As Thou Wilt"

"Great Is Thy Faithfulness"

"Guide Me, O Thou Great Jehovah"

"Jesus Loves Me" (for a child)

"Jesus Loves Even Me" (for a child)

"Saviour, Like a Shepherd Lead Us"

"Holy Spirit, Faithful Guide"

"Breathe on Me, Breath of God"

"Holy Ghost, with Light Divine"

"This Is My Father's World"

"The Lord's Prayer"

"The Twenty-Third Psalm"

"What a Friend We Have in Jesus"

"O Love of God Most Full"

"Have Thine Own Way, Lord"

"O Master, Let Me Walk with Thee"

"Must Jesus Bear the Cross Alone"

"Rock of Ages, Cleft for Me"

Appropriate Poems

Crossing the Bar

Sunset and evening star,
    And one clear call for me!
And may there be no moaning of the bar,
    When I put out to sea.

But such a tide as moving seems asleep,
   Too full for sound and foam,
When that which drew from out the boundless deep
   Turns again home.

Twilight and evening bell,
   And after that the dark!
And may there be no sadness of farewell,
   When I embark;

For tho' from out our bourne of Time and Place
   The flood may bear me far,
I hope to see my Pilot face to face
   When I have crossed the bar.

               ALFRED LORD TENNYSON

He Is Not Dead

  He is not dead—this friend—not dead,
  But in the path we mortals tread,
  Got some few trifling steps ahead,
    And nearer to the end;
  So that you, too, once past the bend,
  Shall meet again, as face to face, this friend
    You fancy dead.

               ROBERT LOUIS STEVENSON

Death

Death, be not proud, though some have called thee
Mighty and dreadful, for thou art not so:

For those whom thou think'st thou dost overthrow
Die not, poor Death; nor yet canst thou kill me.
From rest and sleep, which but thy picture be,
Much pleasure; then from thee much more must
    flow;
And soonest our best men with thee do go—
Rest of their bones and souls' delivery!
Thou'rt slave to fate, chance, kings, and desperate
    men,
And dost with poison, war, and sickness dwell;
And poppy or charms can make us sleep as well
And better than thy stroke. Why swell'st thou then?
    One short sleep past, we wake eternally,
    And Death shall be no more: Death, thou shalt
      die!
                           JOHN DONNE

The Eternal Goodness

Yet, in the maddening maze of things,
    And tossed by storm and flood,
To one fixed trust my spirit clings;
    I know that God is good!

. . . .

I long for household voices gone,
    For vanished smiles I long,
But God hath led my dear ones on,
    And He can do no wrong.

I know not what the future hath
   Of marvel or surprise,
Assured alone that life and death
   His mercy underlies.

And if my heart and flesh are weak
   To bear an untried pain,
The bruised reed He will not break,
   But strengthen and sustain.

And so beside the Silent Sea
   I wait the muffled oar;
No harm from Him can come to me
   On ocean or on shore.

I know not where His islands lift
   Their fronded palms in air;
I only know I cannot drift
   Beyond His love and care.

And Thou, O Lord, by whom are seen
   Thy creatures as they be,
Forgive me if too close I lean
   My human heart on Thee!
             JOHN GREENLEAF WHITTIER

Strong Son of God

Strong Son of God, immortal Love,
   Whom we, that have not seen thy face,

By faith, and faith alone, embrace,
Believing where we cannot prove; . . .
. . . .
Thou wilt not leave us in the dust;
Thou madest man, he knows not why;
He thinks he was not made to die;
And thou hast made him; thou art just.

ALFRED LORD TENNYSON, from "In Memoriam"

Pass Hence

Pass hence, beloved, at the call divine,
Leaving the path we twain have trod;
Pass, and the soul that still is one with thine
Through grief shall learn the way to God.

*An inscription in one of the catacombs at Rome,
translated by* GILBERT MURRAY

Yet Love Will Dream

Yet love will dream, and Faith will trust,
(Since he who knows our need is just)
That somehow, somewhere, meet we must.
Alas for him who never sees
The stars shine through his cypress trees!
Who, hopeless, lays his dead away,
Nor looks to see the breaking day
Across the mournful marble play!

Who hath not learned, in hours of faith,
   The truth to flesh and sense unknown,
That Life is ever Lord of Death,
   And Love can never lose its own!
                          JOHN GREENLEAF WHITTIER

High Flight

Oh! I have slipped the surly bonds of earth
   And danced the skies on laughter-silvered wings;
Sunward I've climbed, and joined the tumbling
      mirth
   Of sun-split clouds—and done a hundred things
You have not dreamed of—wheeled and soared
      and swung
   High in the sunlit silence. Hov'ring there,
I've chased the shouting wind along, and flung
   My eager craft through footless halls of air. . . .

Up, up the long, delirious, burning blue
   I've topped the wind-swept heights with easy
      grace
Where never lark, or even eagle flew—
   And, while with silent lifting mind I've trod
The high untrespassed sanctity of space,
   Put out my hand, and touched the face of God.
                          JOHN GILLESPIE MAGEE, JR.*

---

* The author, a pilot in the Royal Canadian Air Force, died
in action in 1942.

Be Still

Be still, my soul: the Lord is on thy side;
  Bear patiently the cross of grief or pain;
Leave to thy God to order and provide;
  In every change He faithful will remain.
Be still, my soul: thy best, thy heavenly Friend
Through thorny ways leads to a joyful end.

Be still, my soul: thy God doth undertake
  To guide the future as he has the past.
Thy hope, thy confidence let nothing shake;
  All now mysterious shall be bright at last.
Be still, my soul: the waves and winds will know

His voice who ruled them while he dwelt below.
Be still, my soul: the hour is hastening on
  When we shall be for ever with the Lord,
When disappointment, grief, and fear are gone,
  Sorrow forgot, love's purest joys restored.
Be still, my soul: when change and tears are past,
All safe and blessed we shall meet at last.

KATHARINA VON SCHLEGEL

Answered Prayer

God answers prayer; sometimes when hearts are
    weak
He gives the very gifts believers seek.

But often faith must learn a deeper rest,
And trust God's silence when he does not speak;
 For, he whose name is Love will send the best.
Stars may burn out, nor mountain walls endure,
But God is true, his promises are sure
 To those who seek.

MYRA GOODWIN PLANTZ

In Pastures Green

In pastures green? Not always; sometimes He
Who knoweth best, in kindness leadeth me
In weary ways, where heavy shadows be.

. . . .

And by still waters? No, not always so;
Ofttimes the heavy tempests round me blow,
And o'er my soul the waves and billows go.

But when the storms beat loudest, and I cry
Aloud for help, the Master standeth by,
And whispers to my soul, "Lo, it is I."

. . . .

So, where He leads me I can safely go,
And in the blest hereafter I shall know
Why in His wisdom He hath led me so.

H. H. BARRY

Along the Road

I walked a mile with Pleasure,
 She chattered all the way,

But left me none the wiser
   For all she had to say.

I walked a mile with Sorrow,
   And ne'er a word said she;
But oh, the things I learned from her
   When Sorrow walked with me!

                    ROBERT BROWNING HAMILTON

E'en for the dead I will not bind
   My soul to grief—death cannot long divide:
For is it not as if the rose that climbed
   My garden wall had blossomed on the other
      side?
Death doth hide but not divide;
   Beloved, thou art on Christ's other side.

                    AUTHOR AND TITLE UNKNOWN

On the Death of Joseph Rodman Drake

   Green be the turf above thee,
      Friend of my better days!
   None knew thee but to love thee,
      None named thee but to praise.

                    FITZ-GREENE HALLECK

Faith and Sight

So I go on not knowing,
   —I would not, if I might—

I would rather walk in the dark with God
    Than go alone in the light;
I would rather walk with Him by faith
    Than walk alone by sight.

MARY G. BRAINARD

Nightfall

Fold up the tent!
The sun is in the West.
Tomorrow my untented soul will range
Among the blest.
    And I am well content,
    For what is sent, is sent,
    And God knows best.

. . . .

Fold up the tent!
Above the mountain's crest,
I hear a clear voice calling, calling clear,—
"To rest! To rest!"
    And I am glad to go,
    For the sweet oil is low,
    And rest is best!

JOHN OXENHAM

The Open Door

You, my son,
Have shown me God.
Your kiss upon my cheek

Has made me feel the gentle touch
Of Him who leads us on.
The memory of your smile, when young,
Reveals His face,
As mellowing years come on apace.
And when you went before,
You left the gates of heaven ajar
That I might glimpse,
Approaching from afar,
The glories of His grace.
Hold, son, my hand,
Guide me along the path,
That, coming,
I may stumble not,
Nor roam,
Nor fail to show the way
Which leads us—home.

GRACE COOLIDGE

He Giveth His Beloved Sleep

Of all the thoughts of God that are
Borne inward unto souls afar,
Along the Psalmist's music deep,
Now tell me if that any is,
For gift or grace, surpassing this:
    "He giveth his beloved—sleep"?

. . . .

And friends, dear friends, when it shall be
That this low breath is gone from me,
And round my bier ye come to weep,
Let One, most loving of you all
Say "Not a tear must o'er her fall!
    He giveth his beloved—sleep."
                    ELIZABETH BARRETT BROWNING

When Earth's Last Picture Is Painted

When Earth's last picture is painted
    and the tubes are twisted and dried,
When the oldest colours have faded,
    and the youngest critic has died,
We shall rest, and, faith, we shall need it—
    lie down for an aeon or two,
  Till the Master of All Good Workmen
    shall put us to work anew.

And those that were good shall be happy:
    they shall sit in a golden chair;
They shall splash at a ten-league canvas
    with brushes of comets' hair;
They shall find real saints to draw from—
    Magdalene, Peter, and Paul;
They shall work for an age at a sitting
    and never be tired at all!

And only the Master shall praise us,
   and only The Master shall blame;
And no one shall work for money,
   and no one shall work for fame,
But each for the joy of the working,
   and each, in his separate star,
Shall draw the Thing as he sees It,
   for the God of Things as They Are.

RUDYARD KIPLING

Part V

Organizing a Church

Jesus said, "On this rock I will build my church, and the powers of death shall not prevail against it. I will give you the keys of the kingdom of heaven, and whatever you bind on earth shall be bound in heaven, and whatever you loose on earth shall be loosed in heaven" (Matt. 16:18–19, RSV). Christ created the church; he inaugurated it as an institution; and he commissioned it to fulfil his ministry as set forth in the gospel. Jesus came first to elicit a response from believing men, and also to enlist an organized following of disciples.

His people have been organizing themselves into local churches since the day Christ inaugurated the Christian movement. Paul declared that Christ is the head of the church, his body—and its Saviour. He "loved the church and gave himself up for her, that he might sanctify her, having cleansed her by the washing of water with the word, that the church might be presented before him in splendor, without spot or wrinkle or any such thing, that she might be holy and without blemish" (Eph. 5:25–27, RSV).

The following guiding principles, suggested procedures, and suggested order of service are meant to provide aid in organizing a new church.

Guiding Principles

1. The New Testament speaks of the church as a spiritual fellowship of redeemed persons (the people of God, the entire body of Christ), and as a functioning institution (local), at least loosely organized.

2. The church must be organized in order effectively to implement the mission given by its head, the Lord Jesus Christ. The New Testament sets forth general principles for organization and function, but does not give exacting details.

3. The local church as institution is first of all a fellowship of persons and secondarily a representative group of the whole "people of God."

4. A local church is at the same time autonomous in its government and responsible to the wider fellowship of believers, the kingdom of God.

5. Churches as institutions or organizations are mutually interdependent in fulfilling the mission received from the Lord. This is the root principle of the denomination, composed of local churches voluntarily working together in the promotion of God's kingdom.

6. Any group of Christians may organize a church without the authority of any other existing church; however, it is practical for them to seek the cooperation and approval of some existing organization when possible.

7. Voluntariness under the lordship of Christ is the basic principle by which churches agree to work together in carrying out the Great Commission.

8. The New Testament assumes the need for leaders in the church. It speaks specifically of pastors and

deacons and implies the need for other leaders, such as ministers and teachers. These offices of leadership are functional and not ecclesiastical.

Suggested Procedure

There are usually three situations out of which arises the need for organizing a new church. (1) An existing church may recognize the need for establishing a mission which may gradually mature and desire to become an independent, functioning church. (2) A group of Christians in a given community, not representative of any particular church, may see the need for organizing a church. (3) A group in an existing church, feeling they can no longer agree in doctrine and/or practice with the church, may seek to form a new church in a separate location. As in the case of Paul and Barnabas, they agree to function independently of each other.

1. A group desiring to organize a new church should be deliberate in considering the need and desirability of a new church. Factors to consider are (1) whether the interests of God's kingdom could be better served by the establishment of a new church; (2) whether the population and economic strength of the community could support a new church; and (3) whether the proximity of location to other churches of similar faith and practice would make a new church impractical.

2. The group should confer with leaders of existing churches and with denominational leaders in the area on the advisability of organizing another church, and obtain their approval and cooperation if possible. If there is a sponsoring church, its congregation should

vote formally to approve the organization and to pledge its prayers and support to the new church.

3. Agreement having been reached that a church should be organized, a time and place for the service of organization should be announced publicly.

4. An invitation should be sent to all persons interested in becoming members of the church and a fraternal invitation sent to the members of the sponsoring church, to appropriate representatives of other churches, and to denominational leadership.

5. An order of service should be planned in detail for the organization of the new church. Actually, it should be an act of worship since the church is committed to the will of God for the fulfilment of his kingdom. There being no set order for such a service, there is room for creativity appropriate to the particular occasion. The following suggested order may serve as a guide.

Order of Service

CALL TO WORSHIP

MINISTER: O come, let us worship and bow down: let us kneel before the Lord our maker [*Psalm 95:6, KJV*].
CONGREGATION: For he is our God; and we are the people of his pasture, and the sheep of his hand [*v.7*].
MINISTER: No other foundation can any one lay than that which is laid, which is Jesus Christ [*1 Cor. 3:11, RSV*].
CONGREGATION:[God] has made him the head over

all things for the church, which is his body, the fulness of him who fills all in all [*Eph. 1:22–23,RSV*].

HYMN OF ADORATION—"O Worship the King"; "Praise, My Soul, the King of Heaven"; "To God Be the Glory"; or some other

INVOCATION

STATEMENT BY A PARTICIPANT

This will include the purpose of the meeting, the reading of the sponsoring church's approval and agreement to send forth members to do the work of Christ, and the reading of a resolution that the congregation enter into the organization of a church. Such a resolution may read as follows: "Resolved, that we who are assembled in the name of our Lord Jesus Christ, believing that it is God's will for us to establish a church, do solemnly enter into covenant to become an organized fellowship for the purpose of worshiping God, witnessing to his saving grace, living as Christians in the world, and ministering to the needs of people wherever we observe such needs, to the glory of God the Father, the Son, and the Holy Spirit."

The resolution may then be voted on by the congregation.

THE READING OF THE SCRIPTURES—Matthew 16:13–28; 28:18–20; John 15:1–17; Acts 1:1–8; 2:37–47; Romans 12:1–13; 1 Corinthians 12; 13; Ephesians 4:1–6; Colossians 3:1–17; Hebrews 10:19–25; 1 Peter 2:1–10; or others.

HYMN OF AFFIRMATION—"I Love Thy Kingdom, Lord"; "The Church's One Foundation"; or other

SERMON

A brief sermon on the church and a charge to the new congregation and to the sponsoring church (if any) may be given. The sermon may be omitted.

ROLL CALL

The names of those who have indicated a desire to become part of the new church should be read. These persons will stand and remain standing for the reading of the church covenant.

READING OF THE COVENANT

Let the members standing repeat the Church Covenant, a printed form of which should be provided. See pages 146-48 for suggested covenants.

PRAYER OF DEDICATION AND COMMITMENT

FURTHER BUSINESS

The covenanting group may wish to (1) adopt the articles of faith (see pages 149-150); (2) adopt a constitution and by-laws (see Gaines S. Dobbins, *The Churchbook*, pages 10–24), or appoint a committee to write one; (3) vote to incorporate (required by some states); and (4) call a pastor. Some or all of these matters may be left for a later meeting.

HYMN OF DEDICATION—"Lead On, O King Eternal"; "Onward Christian Soldiers"; "Forward Through the Ages"; "God of Grace and God of Glory"; or some other.

BENEDICTION

The members of the new church may sign the roll of membership during or following the service.

Part VI

Ordination Services

The term "ordain," as it is ordinarily used in the ecclesiastical sense, never occurs in the New Testament. The Greek word translated "ordain" in the King James Version is better translated "appoint." When Jesus said, "Ye have not chosen me, but I have chosen you, and ordained you" (John 15:16,KJV), he used a word meaning to "appoint" or "place" or "set." Paul and Barnabas "appointed" elders in the churches (Acts 14:23). In both the Old Testament and the New Testament leaders were "set apart" in a special way. The "laying on of hands" or the "lifting up of hands" as in invoking a blessing upon someone was a biblical practice. New Testament examples include Acts 6:6; 13:3; 1 Timothy 4:14; and 2 Timothy 1:6. In the third chapter of 1 Timothy Paul speaks of the offices of bishop and deacon. He perhaps implies that church leaders were set apart to these offices. The term "bishop" may be translated pastor or minister in modern terminology. Some churches with a multiple staff of ministers include the pastor or senior minister, the minister of education, and the minister of music in the same category.

Although the New Testament does not teach that ordination is an essential requirement for equipping leaders for their ministry, the ceremony seems in no way to conflict with New Testament principles. The practice of ordination appears to be practical for the organized work of the churches. To make of ordination a sacramental or hierarchical rite is to violate the principles of New Testament theology. Church offices are functional and not ecclesiastical. Ordination symbolizes God's call to ministry, the candidate's commitment of himself to the ministry in the will of God, and the church's approval of the candidate for the ministry. Based upon New Testament teaching and practice, the following guiding principles and procedures are suggested.

Guiding Principles

1. Ordination may be defined as the act by the church in a ceremony of worship of setting one apart to an office of leadership in the Christian ministry.

2. The responsibility for ordination rests with the church, God's people. The functioning church is represented by the local congregation, but it is related to God's people as a whole and should not be exclusive.

3. Ordination is an act of commitment in the presence of God's people on the part of the individual who feels God has called him to minister in a full-time church-related vocation.

4. On the part of the church this ceremony is an act of approval, not an act of bestowal. It is an acknowledgment that God has bestowed certain gifts and has called the individual to service. It symbolizes what God has already done as a work of grace in the life of the person called. Ordination does not impart any rights or qualifications which God has not already bestowed.

5. The church should not be hasty in ordaining an individual. It should be certain that he has the qualifications to serve in the office whether it be as pastor, as deacon, or as any other leader. The candidate should first prove himself to be qualified in character and in gifts for such ministry.

6. Once an individual has been ordained, he should live an exemplary Christian life and show himself to be a maturing leader in the service of Christ. He is responsible primarily to Jesus Christ as Lord and secondarily to the church in functioning as a leader and his behaviour should reflect his sense of responsibility.

The Ordination of Ministers

Ordination to the Christian ministry is interpreted variously, since the New Testament is not specific at this point. Some churches limit the office of minister to that of pastor or to the preaching ministry. Others include a plurality of ministers: the pastor or senior minister, the minister of education, the minister of music, the full-time teacher of religion, the full-time evangelist, and others. Such decisions should be left to the local church and not become a test of fellowship or of doctrinal purity. In the case of the multiple staff ministry, ordination may or may not designate the specific, functional roles of the individuals. Specific roles must be defined in a practical manner as a basis for smooth functioning of the church. Ordination does not bestow any honor or authority on one above another. The New Testament doctrine of the priesthood of believers would preclude this idea in ordination.

Suggested Procedure

The following suggested procedures are based upon New Testament principles, the history of various denominations, and traditional practices in contemporary times. Steps and procedures will vary somewhat according to the denominational patterns and local customs.

1. A candidate for the ministry is usually licensed sometime prior to the request for ordination. When one indicates to the church that he believes God has called him to the ministry, if the church agrees with him, it is appropriate for the church to give him its tentative approval by licensing him to serve until he has proved himself qualified for ordination. This usually includes students who are in preparation for the ministry, but may sometimes include older men who desire to proceed in the ministry without further training. (See page 151 for a suggested form of license.)

2. The candidate himself may approach the pastor of his church with a request to be ordained. Or, the church where he is serving as pastor may make the request of his home church. Or, the pastor of a candidate in training for the ministry may request the home church to ordain him.

3. Upon request the church will authorize the appointment of an advisory council to examine the candidate as to his fitness for ordination. A council usually includes ministers and may also include deacons and/or other church members as desired. There is no biblical basis for limiting the examining council to ordained ministers. Since a minister will likely serve churches

other than the one ordaining him, it is appropriate to invite persons from other churches of like faith and order and perhaps certain denominational leaders to participate in the examining council.

4. The council should be given plenty of time to procure information and to ascertain the qualifications of the candidate. The church should not set a time for ordination until it receives the report from the advisory council. A church should never assume that a council will approve a candidate. Otherwise there would be no point to having an examination of the candidate.

5. When the examining council meets, it may proceed as follows: (1) The council will organize itself by electing a moderator or chairman (usually, but not necessarily, the pastor of the ordaining church), a clerk or secretary, and one to lead in the examination of the candidate. These matters may be left to the pastor. (2) The examination of the candidate should include an evaluation of

—the candidate's statement of his conversion, his call to preach, and his Christian experience in general;

—his doctrinal views on the Bible as God's revelation;

—his views concerning the church;

—his knowledge of the Bible and of denominational history and practice;

—his personal attitudes toward the church, the denomination, and the kingdom of God in general;

—his acquaintance with contemporary thought and affairs;

—the candidate's skills in preaching, teaching, and pastoral ministries;

—his ability to relate to other persons in teamwork and life relationships;

—his evangelistic and missionary commitments;

—his theory and practice of stewardship;

—his attitude toward his community and other denominations; and

—his commitment to the lordship of Jesus Christ in his own life.

The examination should be kept on a high level and deal with basic Christian doctrines and attitudes, and should never degenerate into a debate between individuals on the council concerning nonessential or speculative matters. (3) The examination having been concluded, the council will dismiss the candidate and enter a period of discussion regarding their decision. After discussion and prayer they will decide to recommend either (a) ordination, (b) deferment for a stated period so that the candidate may become better qualified and prepared, or (c) rejection of the application.

6. The secretary of the council should deliver without delay a written notice to the church concerning the council's decision.

7. If the council recommends to proceed with the ordination, the church will then set a time for the ordination service and instruct the pastor to prepare the order of service and to invite the council and others, if it is deemed desirable, to participate in the ordination service.

Order of Service

This suggested order of service may be incorporated

into a regular Sunday morning or evening worship service of the church, or it may be planned for a special time—whichever seems more appropriate. In any event the service should be conducted in a genuine spirit of worship.

CALL TO WORSHIP

MINISTER: Rejoice in the Lord, O you righteous!

CONGREGATION: Praise befits the upright.

MINISTER: For the word of the Lord is upright;

CONGREGATION: And all his work is done in faithfulness.

HYMN OF PRAISE

"Oh, For a Thousand Tongues". . . . . . . Azmon

INVOCATION

AN INTRODUCTORY STATEMENT

MINISTER: We are assembled in the name of our Lord, at the request of this church, and as representatives of the fellowship of churches that have been invited, that we may set aside and ordain A—— to the office and work of the Christian ministry.

(A further word may be said as to the particular field which the candidate plans to enter: the pastorate, ministry of religious education, ministry of music, professional evangelism, missions, teacher of religion, or other work.)

THE READING OF THE SCRIPTURES

The following are some of the passages which will be found suitable: Gen. 12:1–4,7–8; Ex. 3:1–10; Num.

11:16,17,24–30; 1 Sam. 3:1–10,18 to 4:1; 1 Kings 19:9–16; Psalms 19:1–4,7–14; 119:97–112; Isa. 6: 1–8; 40:1–11; 61:1–3,10–11; Jer. 1:4–10; Ezek. 33: 1–9; Matt. 4:12–22; 5:1–16; 9:35 to 10:14,24–25, 40–42; 28:16–20; Luke 10:1–22; John 10:1–18; 15:1–27; 21:15–22; Acts 13:1–3,46–52; Rom. 10: 1–17; 12; 1 Cor. 12; 13; 2 Cor. 4; 5:11–21; 6:1–10; Eph. 3:7–13; 4:1–16; 6:10–20; Phil. 4:8–13; Col. 1:24–29; 1 Tim. 3:1–7; 6:6–16; 2 Tim. 1:1–14; 2:1–15; 4:1–8; James 1 to 2:8,12; 1 Peter 5:1–11; 2 Peter 3:10–18; 1 John 1:1–9; Rev. 1:1–6; 19:1–16; 22:12–20.

HYMN OF AFFIRMATION (or anthem by the choir)

"The Church's One Foundation". . . . . . Aurolia

THE SERMON

The Scripture references above will suggest many texts and themes for the ordination sermon.

CHARGE TO CANDIDATE

(A formal charge to the candidate may or may not be given. It may simply be included as part of the sermon. If a charge is given, it should be formal and brief. The following is offered as a suggestion.)

MINISTER: Do you promise to walk worthily of the vocation to which you are called, seeking always to bring honor to the name of Jesus Christ as your Lord; and do you promise diligently and faithfully to perform the duties of a minister of the gospel with no thought of personal reward or honor, having as your primary motives the winning of persons to Jesus Christ as Saviour and Lord and the building up of the church of Christ through inspiration, teaching, exhortation, and stewardship, to the glory of God? Do you so promise?

CANDIDATE: I promise by the grace of God to try so to live and minister that I may bring honor and glory to the name of Jesus Christ our Lord. [*Or, he may simply say, "I do."*]

MINISTER: You will please kneel for the prayer of ordination and the laying on of hands. [*Candidate will kneel facing the congregation.*]

ORDINATION PRAYER

The prayer should express thanksgiving to God for his calling and invoke his blessings upon the candidate, upon the congregation present, and upon the entire church of the Lord.

THE LAYING ON OF HANDS

The candidate will remain kneeling while those who have been designated by the church file by and place their hands upon his head. These may include ordained ministers only, or ministers and deacons, or others representative of the congregation and designated by the church; or, if it seems practical, the entire congregation may file by and lay on hands. It should be remembered that those who lay hands on the candidate are representing the church and are not acting of themselves in any priestly or hierarchical sense.

CHARGE TO CHURCH

(A formal charge to the church may or may not be given. It may be included in the sermon. In case a charge is given, it should be brief and formal, such as the following.)

MINISTER: Do you, the members of the church, acknowledge and approve A_____ as a minister of the church of Jesus Christ; and will you pray for him in his ministry, and work together with him to accomplish the mission of the church, giving him all due honor and support in his leadership to which the Lord has called him, to the glory and honor of God? If so you will signify your assent by standing [*or raising your hands*].

PRESENTATION OF BIBLE (or money with which to purchase a Bible of the candidate's own choosing)

HYMN OF COMMITMENT—"Jesus, I My Cross Have Taken"; "God of Grace and God of Glory"; "O Jesus, I Have Promised"; "Am I a Soldier of the Cross"; "Make Me a Blessing"; or some other appropriate hymn.

BENEDICTION

If it seems appropriate, the candidate may be asked to lead in a closing prayer.

HAND OF FELLOWSHIP

It is appropriate for the entire congregation to extend a hand of fellowship to the newly ordained minister and his wife if he is married.

The Ordination of Deacons

The office of deacon is generally considered to have originated in the election of the seven as helpers to the apostles (Acts 6:1–6), although they were not called deacons. Some people have regarded the election of the seven as a temporary measure to meet the existing emergency, and claim that they had no successors in a permanent office. Most churches, however, have recognized the need for such an office, due to the similar service needed continually in the churches as implied by Paul in 1 Timothy. Many churches have made it a practice to ordain deacons, although some simply acknowledge them as leaders in the church by a simple service of dedication or commitment.

Guiding Principles

1. The term deacon in the New Testament means minister or servant.

2. As is true of the office of minister or pastor, the office of deacon is not a hierarchical office. No spiritual graces and no particular authority are bestowed in the act of ordination.

3. The office of deacon is one of example, as are all other positions of leadership in the church. Only men who measure up to the scriptural qualifications mentioned in Acts 6:1–6 and 1 Timothy 3:8–13 should be considered for the office.

4. Deacons should be selected from among men who have proved themselves faithful to Christ and the Christian calling in the ministry of the church.

5. Deacons are to be selected and ordained by the church according to the need for their services and the availability of men qualified for the office. It is better not to elect deacons unless there are men qualified for leadership.

6. The number of deacons will depend upon the size of the church and its needs. In the very small church, there might not be enough men available to warrant a deaconship. If they are available, five to seven might be sufficient. In the larger churches it has been found practical to have one deacon for every twenty-five or every fifty members.

7. The length of service of a deacon is not set forth in the New Testament. Many churches consider it appropriate to elect a deacon to office for a particular period of time. Churches have found a rotation system practical. Deacons are divided into multiples of three, one group serving one year, another two years, and another three years when the rotation system is inaugurated. When a deacon completes his term of service, one year elapses before he is eligible to be elected again to the active office. As deacons finish their terms of service, other deacons are elected by the church to fill the vacant offices. These may be men who have previously served or other men to be ordained.

8. The duties of deacons include responsibility for the temporal affairs of the church, the pastoral care and counseling of sick and needy members, and working with the pastor in implementing the general work of the church in both its vast material and spiritual areas.

Suggested Procedure

The following steps of procedure have been found helpful in the election and ordination of deacons.

1. The church will select a representative committee for the nomination of deacons.

2. The congregation may be given the opportunity of suggesting to the committee by secret ballot the names of men who may be considered for the deaconship.

3. The committee will consider men on the basis of requirements and qualifications established by the church. They should have personal interviews with those they deem qualified for the office.

4. The men interviewed should be asked if they would be willing to serve as deacons should the church elect them.

5. The committee will present to the church a list of the men who have been deemed qualified to serve and the number to be elected.

6. After prayer the congregation will write down as many names as there are places. The vote should be taken by secret ballot.

7. The men receiving the largest number of votes will be declared elected to the office.

8. The time for ordination and induction into office will be set. The ordination of deacons is usually conducted in a regular worship service of the church.

Order of Service

CALL TO WORSHIP

HYMN OF PRAISE

"Come, Thou Almighty King". . . . . Trinity

INVOCATION

SCRIPTURE READING

The following passages may be appropriate: Acts 6: 1–7; 1 Tim. 3:1–13; Rom. 12; 1 Cor. 12; Eph. 4: 1–16. Certain passages among those suggested for the ordination of ministers may also be used.

ANTHEM OR OTHER SPECIAL MUSIC

OFFERING

HYMN OF AFFIRMATION

"I Love Thy Kingdom, Lord". . . . . . St. Thomas

SERMON

ACT OF ORDINATION

This is a statement by the minister and an introduction of the candidates to the congregation. They may or may not be asked to tell of their conversion experience, as deemed best.

CHARGE TO THE DEACONS

MINISTER: [*to the candidates who are asked to stand*] Do you promise to strive to so live that you may honor Christ by your life; and do you promise, in the presence of this congregation, to accept the responsibility of the office of deacon in this church, and to the best of your knowledge and ability to discharge all duties of this office?

CANDIDATE: I do.

ORDINATION PRAYER

The candidates are asked to kneel facing the congregation and to remain kneeling after the prayer.

THE LAYING ON OF HANDS

The pastor, ordained deacons, and others whom the church may select, or the entire congregation will file by and lay hands upon the heads of the men.

CHARGE TO THE CHURCH

MINISTER: [*to the congregation*] Do you, members of this congregation, acknowledge these men as deacons in the church; do you promise to encourage and pray for them in their office and to cooperate with them in the fulfilment of the mission of the church? If you do, you will so indicate by rising.

HYMN OF COMMITMENT

"Stand Up, Stand Up for Jesus" (or some other appropriate hymn)

BENEDICTION

HAND OF FELLOWSHIP BY THE CONGREGATION

Deacons' wives may be asked to stand with them to receive the hand of fellowship.

Part VII

Services of Dedication and Installation

It is fitting for Christians to dedicate themselves and their possessions to God. Acts of dedication may be performed in private by the individual, by the family or other small groups, or in public services of dedication by the entire congregation. The choice of appropriate Scripture passages, music, prayers, and other materials can contribute to the effectiveness of the occasion. A certain amount of formal planning and order is essential. All such services should be conducted with dignity and reverence in keeping with the worship of God. To this end the following suggestions are offered.

Guiding Principles

1. All persons rightfully belong to God; they are truly his only when they willingly commit themselves to him. Paul said, "Ye, are not your own, . . . Ye are bought with a price: therefore glorify God in your body, and in your spirit, which are God's" (1 Cor. 6:19–20,KJV).

2. Throughout history God's people have practiced dedication of themselves and their possessions. Biblical examples include: (1) altars—Numbers 7:10–11; (2) silver and gold—2 Samuel 8:11; (3) vessels of service —1 Kings 7:51; (4) the temple of worship—1 Kings 8:63; Ezra 6:16; (5) the wall of Jerusalem—Nehe-

miah 12:27; (6) private dwellings—Deuteronomy 20:
5; (7) persons: Aaron—Exodus 28:3; Samuel—1 Samuel 1:21–28; Saul—1 Samuel 10:1; priests—Ezra
8:23–30; Jesus—Luke 2:22–35; Paul and Barnabas—
Acts 13:2–3; servants (deacons)—Acts 6:1–6; Timothy—2 Timothy 1:3–7.

3. Dedication services are definite acts of worship
and should be planned so as to bring honor to God and
solemn commitment of persons and things to his service.

4. There are no set forms or ceremonies which must
be followed. There is room for variety and creativity to
suit the particular occasion. With serious planning, services and ceremonies can be open to the spirit of God
and may provide transforming experiences.

Dedication of a Church Building

ORGAN PRELUDE

CALL TO WORSHIP

> Lift up your heads, O gates!
>> And be lifted up, O ancient doors!
>> That the King of glory may come in.
> Who is the King of glory?
>> The Lord, strong and mighty, . . .
>> The Lord of hosts,
>> He is the King of glory!
>>>> [*Psalm 24:7–10, RSV*]

HYMN OF PRAISE—"Rejoice, the Lord Is King"; "All
   Hail the Power of Jesus' Name"; or another

INVOCATION

THE READING OF THE SCRIPTURES

   1 Kings 8:54–61; 9:1–3; 2 Chronicles 6:1–2,4,14,

17–20, 39–41; Psalm 84; 96; 122; Matthew 21:12–16; John 2:13–17; 1 Corinthians 3:9–23; Ephesians 2:13–22; 1 Peter 2:4–10; or others

PRESENTATION OF THE BUILDING

MINISTER: Fellow Christians, we are assembled here in the name of our Lord who has blessed the work of our hands in the raising of this building [*sanctuary*] as a house of worship. I now recognize the chairman of the building committee who will present the building to the congregation.

CHAIRMAN: Brother Pastor [*Dr.____*], on behalf of the building committee, the architect, the contractors, and all who have participated in the erection of this building, I now present the keys as a symbol of this entire structure as we proceed in its dedication to our Lord.

MINISTER: Since it has pleased the Lord to bless his people in the building of this house for use in his service, let us now dedicate it to the honor of his holy name.

LITANY OF DEDICATION

MINISTER: How amiable are thy tabernacles, O Lord of hosts! Except the Lord build the house, they labor in vain who build it.

CONGREGATION: Bless the Lord, O my soul, and all that is within me, bless his holy name.

MINISTER: To the glory of God the Father, who has called us by his grace; God the Son, who loved us and gave himself for us; God the Holy Spirit, who illumines and strengthens us,

CONGREGATION: To thee, O Lord, we dedicate this house;

MINISTER: For the worship of God in prayer and praise, for the preaching of the redeeming gospel, for the celebration of the gospel in baptism and the Lord's Supper,

CONGREGATION: We dedicate this house;

MINISTER: For the comfort of all who mourn, for strength to those who are tempted, for light to those who seek the way,

CONGREGATION: We dedicate this house;

MINISTER: For the hallowing of family life, for teaching and guiding the young, for the perfecting of the saints,

CONGREGATION: We dedicate this house;

MINISTER: For the conversion of sinners, for the promotion of righteousness, for the extension of the kingdom of God to the ends of the earth,

CONGREGATION: We dedicate this house;

MINISTER: In the unity of the faith, in the bond of Christian brotherhood, in love and goodwill to all,

CONGREGATION: We dedicate this house;

MINISTER: In gratitude for the labors of all who love and serve this church, in loving remembrance of all those who have finished their labors, in hope of eternal life through Jesus Christ our Lord,

CONGREGATION: We dedicate this house.

MINISTER AND PEOPLE: As members of the body of Christ, grateful for our heritage, and sensible of our responsibility, we now dedicate ourselves to the worship and service of Almighty God in this building and in the world, through Jesus Christ our Lord. Amen.

PRAYER OF DEDICATION

HYMN OF AFFIRMATION—"Faith of Our Fathers," "Glorious Things of Thee are Spoken," "The Church's One Foundation," or others

SERMON

The sermon may be omitted if desired.

HYMN OF DEDICATION—"Jesus Calls Us o'er The Tumult"; "Stand Up, Stand up for Jesus"; "Hark, the Voice of Jesus Calling"; "To the Work"; or others

BENEDICTION

Laying a Cornerstone

This may be a special service or it may follow a regular morning worship service. In the latter case, the following materials may be substituted in the order of worship to fit in.

CALL TO WORSHIP

"Our help is in the name of the Lord, who made heaven and earth. Except the Lord build the house, they labour in vain that build it" (Psalm 124:8; 127:1,KJV).

HYMN OF ADORATION

"The Church's One Foundation"

INVOCATION

READING OF THE SCRIPTURES

1 Corinthians 3:9–16; 1 Peter 2:6–10. See also passages listed under "Dedication of a Building."

HYMN OF AFFIRMATION—"Faith of Our Fathers"

SPECIAL MUSIC

SERMON

Following the sermon the congregation will retire outside the building for the ceremony.

LITANY OF DEDICATION

MINISTER: To the glory of God the Father, to the service of our Master and his church, and to the abiding presence of the Holy Spirit,

CONGREGATION: We lay the cornerstone of this church.

MINISTER: For a building of which Jesus Christ is the chief cornerstone, the pillar and ground of the truth,

CONGREGATION: We lay this cornerstone.

MINISTER: For a building that shall stand as a symbol of his church, whose bond of fellowship is the love of God,

CONGREGATION: We lay this cornerstone.

MINISTER: For a church that seeks to exalt the truth of God through his revealed Word,

CONGREGATION: We lay this cornerstone.

MINISTER: For a church that shall be a renewing and cleansing power in this community,

CONGREGATION: We lay this cornerstone.

MINISTER: For a church that offers to the suffering of the community its ministry of inspiration, comfort, and hope,

CONGREGATION: We lay this cornerstone.

MINISTER: For a church that offers its life to the world of men who are seeking the abundant life,

CONGREGATION: We lay this cornerstone.

MINISTER: In loving memory of those who have departed this earthly life, in dedication to the era in which we live, and as a symbol of our hope in eternal life,

CONGREGATION: We lay this cornerstone.

EXHIBIT OF ARTICLES

Articles to be placed in the cornerstone, such as a Bible, a hymnal, church periodicals, names of leaders, officers, building committee, and so on may be exhibited.

LAYING OF STONE

This will be done by the minister or chairman of the building committee and the builder.

PRAYER OF DEDICATION

HYMN OF PRAISE—"The Doxology" and a choral amen

A Ground-Breaking Ceremony

This may be either of two types of service. One would be a brief ceremony following a regular morning service, where the congregation will move to the location of the building site.

INTRODUCTORY STATEMENT

The minister will give an introductory statement, concerning the purpose and significance of the ceremony, the plans, and other appropriate remarks. This statement may be shared by another leader.

THE TURNING OF THE SOIL

The minister and one or more leaders (chairman of building committee, chairman of deacons, oldest member of the church, a representative of the youth, or any others as seems appropriate for the situation) will take a spade (shovel) and turn a small amount of dirt.

THE PRAYER OF DEDICATION

THE HYMN OF DEDICATION—"All Hail the Power of Jesus' Name"

THE BENEDICTION

The second type of ceremony may be a historic occasion calling for a longer service. The entire service may be conducted at the site out of doors. In that case, chairs should be provided, especially for the older people.

CALL TO WORSHIP

HYMN OF PRAISE—"All Hail the Power of Jesus' Name"

INVOCATION

THE READING OF THE SCRIPTURES (Psalm 24, KJV)

MINISTER: The earth is the Lord's, and the fulness thereof; the world, and they that dwell therein.

CONGREGATION: For he hath founded it upon the seas, and established it upon the floods.

MINISTER: Who shall ascend into the hill of the Lord? or who shall stand in his holy place?

CONGREGATION: He that hath clean hands, and a pure heart; who hath not lifted up his soul unto vanity, nor sworn deceitfully.

MINISTER: He shall receive the blessing from the Lord, and righteousness from the God of his salvation.

CONGREGATION: This is the generation of them that seek him, that seek thy face.

MINISTER: Lift up your heads, O ye gates; and be ye lift up, ye everlasting doors.

CONGREGATION: And the King of glory shall come in.

MINISTER: Who is this King of glory?

CONGREGATION: The Lord strong and mighty, the Lord mighty in battle.

MINISTER: Lift up your heads, O ye gates; even lift them up, ye everlasting doors.

CONGREGATION: And the King of glory shall come in.

MINISTER: Who is this King of glory?

CONGREGATION: The Lord of hosts, he is the King of glory.

STATEMENT OF PURPOSE

This may include the plans for building and other remarks.

HISTORY OF THE CHURCH

This may be a significant statement by some leader in the church.

SPECIAL MUSIC

"Glorious is Thy Name" (by choir) . . . . Mozart

SERMON

This will be delivered by the pastor or a guest leader of the denomination, or it may be omitted if desired.

THE TURNING OF THE SOIL

See suggestions above.

PRAYER OF DEDICATION

HYMN OF COMMITMENT—"Lead On O King Eternal," or another

BENEDICTION

Dedication of a Home

This service is appropriate for the dedication of a family in a new house or at any time. Fellow church members and other friends may be invited to attend the service of dedication of a home. The pastor may also be invited to participate.

CALL TO WORSHIP

Our help is in the name of the Lord, who made heaven and earth [*Psalm 124:8, RSV*]

Unless the Lord builds the house, those who build it labor in vain [*Psalm 127:1, RSV*].

HYMN—"O God, Our Help in Ages Past"; "O Worship the King"; or others

INVOCATION

This may be a brief prayer focusing on the worship of God and asking his blessing on the service.

THE READING OF THE SCRIPTURES

Deuteronomy 6:4–9; Exodus 20:1–21; Psalm 23; 34; 121; Matthew 5:1–16; Luke 10:38–42; 19:1–10 1 Corinthians 13; Ephesians 5:22–33; 6:1–4; Colossians 3:12–21; or other appropriate passages

PRESENTATION OF THE HOME

THE HOST, HUSBAND, OR BOTH HUSBAND AND WIFE: Because it is our desire to dedicate this house and ourselves to God, as we seek to build a Christian home, we present this house for dedication.

MINISTER [*or other leader*]: The home was the first institution God established. It is God's gift to the family and to society. It is the privilege and duty of every family to dedicate their home to God, their

Creator, Redeemer, and Sustainer. This family [couple] is to be commended for thus honoring God. The poet wrote:

So long as there are homes to which men turn
At close of Day;
So long as there are homes where children are,
Where women stay—
If love and loyalty and faith be found
Across those sills—
A stricken nation can recover from
Its gravest ills.

So long as there are homes where fires burn
And there is bread;
So long as there are homes where lamps are lit
And prayers are said;
Although people falter through the dark—
And nations grope—
With God himself back of these little homes—
We have sure hope.

GRACE NOLL CROWELL

CANDLE LIGHTING CEREMONY

Candlelight is a symbol of love and knowledge and cheer. While the wife lights a candle, the husband may say: "The Lord is my light and my salvation; whom shall I fear?" [Psalm 27:1, RSV]. Or,
Jesus spoke to them, saying, "I am the light of the world; he who follows me will not walk in darkness, but will have the light of life" (John 8:12, RSV). Or,

Jesus also said, "You are the light of the world. . . .
Let your light so shine before men, that they may see
your good works and give glory to your Father who
is in heaven" [*Matt. 5:14–16, RSV*].

THE LITANY OF DEDICATION

This litany of dedication may be read by members
of the family only or by all members present, or it
may be read responsively as here outlined.

LEADER [*minister or other*]: With gratitude to God
who has provided the materials and given strength to
the builders who erected this house,

MEMBERS: We dedicate our [*this*] home.

LEADER: To the deep and abiding love which binds
the family together,

MEMBERS: We dedicate our [*this*] home.

LEADER: To the understanding, patience, discipline,
and forgiveness essential for the growth and fulfilment
of persons,

MEMBERS: We dedicate our [*this*] home.

LEADER: To the vision, courage, faith, and hope that
make life cheerful and serene,

MEMBERS: We dedicate our [*this*] home.

LEADER: To the beauty and order and cleanliness
that provide a wholesome atmosphere and elevate
the spirit of Christian living,

MEMBERS: We dedicate our [*this*] home.

LEADER: To the training of the bodies, minds,
and souls of all who live within these walls,

MEMBERS: We dedicate our [*this*] home.

LEADER: To the work of God's kingdom in the world
and in cooperation with his church,

MEMBERS: We dedicate our [*this*] home to the glory of God the Father, Son, and Holy Spirit.

PRAYER OF DEDICATION (by the leader)

The Lord's Prayer (by all persons present)

Our Father which art in heaven, Hallowed be thy name.
Thy kingdom come. Thy will be done in earth as it is in heaven.
Give us this day our daily bread.
And forgive us our debts, as we forgive our debtors.
And lead us not into temptation, but deliver us from evil:
For thine is the kingdom, and the power, and the glory, for ever. Amen [*Matt. 6:9-13, KJV*].

or

Bless This Home (by the family)

Bless, O Lord, this home.
Fill each room with Your Presence.
Teach us anew how to live here without hurting each other by harsh words and unkind actions.
Deepen our trust in one another so that we can honestly accept each other as we are.
Show us that here we do not have to impress.
In such fellowship—help us to know You better so that we in turn may be unafraid to know ourselves.
And as we go back into the world—help us to go forth with Your confidence. Amen.

BLAISE LEVAI

Dedication of Children

This service is actually a promise of parents to offer their child (usually in its infancy) to God, and to dedicate themselves to the rearing of the child for the glory of God. It should be understood that this act of dedication is not a sacrament; it does not impart salvation to the child. Ceremonial acts, such as baptism, the laying on of hands, and so forth, are not appropriate in this service. It is a recognition that the life of the child is a gift from God and an acknowledgment that its life rightfully belongs to God. The dedication of children is taught in the Bible. As a baby, Jesus was dedicated by his parents (Luke 2:22–35). This act of worship has been called the "presentation of the child" (v. 22) and "the blessing of the child" (v. 34), as in Jesus' blessing of the children (Mark 10:16).

The dedication of a child may be performed by the parents at the hospital and/or later in the home. They may invite the pastor to participate. Also, the act of dedication is often part of a Sunday morning worship service, perhaps on Children's Day as a part of Christian Home Week, when parents are invited to bring their babies and small children who have not previously been presented to God. The following suggestions may be adapted for these various occasions. At the appropriate time in a regular worship service, perhaps after the call to worship, opening hymn, and invocation, this order may be followed.

INTRODUCTORY STATEMENT

MINISTER: It is the privilege of the church to

encourage and assist parents in the proper training and development of their children. Therefore, it is appropriate for home and church to
unite in this service of dedication for parents and
child [*children*]. The act of dedication is in
keeping with the teaching of God's Word. An
example is the dedication of Jesus by his parents.

In this service of dedication we are first to
give thanks to God for the creation and birth
of this child [*these children*]. In the second
place, we are to make a solemn promise as parents and as a church that, relying on the grace
of God and working together as home and
church, we will endeavor to provide guidance
for this child [*these children*] in instruction,
discipline, salvation experience, and growth in
the Lord. In the third place, we are to pray for
God's blessings upon this child [*these children*], in the presence of his Spirit, remembering how the Lord Jesus Christ took little children and blessed them.

THE READING OF THE SCRIPTURES

Hear, O Israel: The Lord our God is one
Lord; and you shall love the Lord your God
with all your heart, and with all your soul, and
with all your might. And these words which I

command you this day shall be upon your heart; and you shall teach them diligently to your children, and shall talk of them when you sit in your house, and when you walk by the way, and when you lie down, and when you rise [*Deut. 6:4–7,RSV*].

✳ The steadfast love of the Lord is from everlàsting to everlasting upon those who fear him, and his righteousness to children's children, to those who keep his covenant and remember to do his commandments [*Psalm 103:17–18,RSV*].

✳ And he took a child, and put him in the midst of them; and taking him in his arms, he said to them, "Whoever receives one such child in my name receives me; and whoever receives me, receives not me but him who sent me" [*Mark 9:36–37,RSV*].

Other suitable passages are 1 Samuel 1:24 to 2:1; Psalm 127:1,3; Matthew 18:5,10,14; Mark 10: 13–16; Luke 2:25–40; 9:46–48; 18:15–17; Ephesians 6:1–4; Colossians 3:20–21.

PRESENTATION

MINISTER: We acknowledge Mr. and Mrs.——, who present their son [*daughter*] before God and this company of the church.

(If there is more than one set of parents, the names of all parents and their children should be called.)

THE COMMITMENT

MINISTER TO THE PARENTS: In presenting your child to the Lord, do you promise in dependence upon God's grace and upon the partnership of the church, to teach him the truths of the Christian faith, to set a Christian example before him, to bring him up in the instruction and discipline of the Lord, and to encourage him to accept Christ as his Saviour under the guidance of the Holy Spirit?

PARENTS: We do.

MINISTER TO THE CONGREGATION: Do you, as members of the church, promise to join these parents in the teaching and training of this child that he may be led in due time to trust Christ as Saviour and to confess him in baptism and church membership? If you accept this responsibility, will you indicate it by standing? (*The congregation will stand*).

PRAYER OF DEDICATION

This is a prayer of thanksgiving for the child [*children*], a promise to God to be responsible for him [*them*], and a petition to God for his blessings in leadership in the lives of parents and child [*children*]. The parents will take the children to the nursery and return to the service. The worship service will proceed according to the regular order. It may be desirable to have a special sermon to fit the occasion.

Installation of Church Leaders

An installation service for church leaders is always appropriate and may be quite meaningful. The purpose is the dedication and commitment of elected persons to their offices of responsibility. The services may be designed for the installation of a new pastor, other paid staff members, or volunteer leaders in the various organizations of the church. The following service is designed as a general installation for all church leaders (officers, teachers, and general committees) at the beginning of a new church year. With certain changes it may serve as an order of service for any specific area of leadership.

The service may be included as part of a regular morning worship. At the appropriate place in the worship service, perhaps following the call to worship, hymn of praise, and invocation, this order of installation and dedication may be included. Or, it may follow the sermon as a climax to the worship service.

RECOGNITION OF LEADERS

MINISTER: All Christians are called of God to live, to witness, and to minister for his glory. Church members are called to serve according to their various talents. We now recognize the leaders [*officers, teachers, committee members, and so forth*] who have been elected to serve during the new church year.

(They will be asked to rise, and their names may be called; or they may be presented in printed form, indicating their offices, if the list is too long to call in the service).

THE READING OF THE SCRIPTURES

Jesus said, "Whoever would be great among you must be your servant, and whoever would be first among you must be your slave; even as the Son of man came not to be served but to serve, and to give his life as a ransom for many" [*Matt. 20:26–28,RSV*].

Now you are the body of Christ and individually members of it. And God has appointed in the church first apostles, second prophets, third teachers, then workers of miracles, then healers, helpers, administrators, speakers in various kinds of tongues. Are all apostles? Are all prophets? Are all teachers? Do all work miracles? Do all possess gifts of healing? Do all speak with tongues? Do all interpret? But earnestly desire the higher gifts. And I will show you a still more excellent way. . . . Make love your aim, and earnestly desire the spiritual gifts [*1 Cor. 12:27–31 to 14:1,RSV*].

I . . . beg you to lead a life worthy of the calling to which you have been called, with all low-

liness and meekness, with patience, forbearing
one another in love, eager to maintain the unity
of the Spirit in the bond of peace. . . . his gifts
were that some should be apostles, some prophets, some evangelists, some pastors and teachers,
for the equipment of the saints, for the work of
ministry, for building up the body of Christ,
until we all attain to the unity of the faith and
of the knowledge of the Son of God, to mature
manhood, to the measure of the stature of the
fulness of Christ [*Eph. 4:1–13,RSV*].

Having gifts that differ according to the grace
given to us, let us use them. . . . Never flag in
zeal, be aglow with the Spirit, serve the Lord.
Rejoice in your hope, be patient in tribulation,
be constant in prayer [*Rom. 12:6–12,RSV*].

Whatever you do, in word or deed, do everything in the name of the Lord Jesus, giving
thanks to God the Father through him [*Col.
3:17,RSV*].

OTHER APPROPRIATE PASSAGES
For general use—Matthew 4:23; 9:35–38; 28:18–
20; Mark 1:16–20; 8:34–35; Luke 9:1–2; 10:1–
2,16,20; Romans 12:1–2,6,11–13; 1 Corinthians
13; Ephesians 4:1–8,11–13

For ministers—Isaiah 52:7; 2 Corinthians 4:5–6; 1 Timothy 6:11–16; 2 Timothy 1:6–7; 8–14; 2:14–15; 4:1–5

For teachers—Matthew 5:1–19; 13:18–23; Mark 1: 21–22; Galatians 6:6; 2 Timothy 2:15; 2 Peter 3:18

For youth—Proverbs 3:5–6; Ecclesiastes 12:1,13–14; Matthew 6:19–24,33; Ephesians 6:10–18; 1 Timothy 4:11–16.

For musicians—Psalm 95:1–3; 96:1–10; 98:4–6; 100:1–5; 105:1–4; 150:1–6; Colossians 3:16–17; Revelation 5:11–14; 19:1–6.

(Many of these passages will fit more than one area.)

A LITANY OF COMMITMENT

MINISTER: Because thou hast called us to salvation and to Christian living,

WORKERS: We consecrate ourselves to thee, O Lord.

MINISTER: Because thou hast commanded us to witness to the gospel of saving grace,

WORKERS: We consecrate our lips to thee, O Lord.

MINISTER: Because thou hast commanded us to teach the unsearchable riches of thy Word.

WORKERS: We consecrate our minds to thee, O Lord.

MINISTER: Because thou hast called us to minister to people wherever we find them in need,

WORKERS: We dedicate our hands in thy service, O Lord.

MINISTER: Because we are so often limited in our understanding,

WORKERS: We plead the direction of thy Holy Spirit, O Lord.

MINISTER: Because the work we face is often unpleasant and difficult,

WORKERS: Make us constant in our work, O Lord.

MINISTER: Because our sins of selfishness often lead to misunderstanding and wrong attitudes,

WORKERS: Wilt thou keep our hearts pure, O Lord.

MINISTER: Because of the magnitude of the opportunity to challenge and mold the lives of others,

WORKERS: Help us to reflect the character of Christ in our living and service, O Lord.

ALL: We beseech thee, O Lord, to use our ministry for the edifying of the body of Christ, the church, until we all come in the unity of the faith, and of the knowledge of Jesus Christ thy Son, unto mature Christian workers, unto the measure of the stature of the fulness of Christ.

PRAYER OF CONSECRATION

The minister may or may not lead the main prayer.

ALL: Let the words of our mouths and the meditations of our hearts be acceptable in thy sight, O Lord, our strength and our redeemer.

HYMN OF COMMITMENT

"Jesus I My Cross Have Taken"; "Lord, Speak to Me, That I May Speak"; "O Jesus, I Have Promised"; "O Master, Let Me Walk with Thee"; "Beneath the Cross of Jesus"; "I Love to Tell the Story"

BENEDICTION

The following scriptural benedictions are appropriate: 2 Thessalonians 2:16; Hebrews 13:20; Jude 24–25.

Part VIII

Visitation and Counseling

The ministry of shepherding or the care of souls is a major area of the church's ministry. All church members as a fellowship of the concerned are responsible for one another. Jesus himself "went about doing good." He gave support and guidance which produced healing for troubled people. The modern pastor must also invest a great deal of time in visitation and counseling with burdened people—the sick and dying, the grieving, the shut-in, the elderly, the anxious and fearful, the guilt-ridden, the unbelieving, the forsaken. This will require wise use of his time and a knowledge of spiritual resources in meeting people's needs. The following principles and materials are meant to aid him and other church members in performing this ministry.

Guiding Principles

1. The minister is a pastor-preacher. His preaching should encourage people to seek his counsel as a pastor.

2. The pastor should organize, train, and encourage the laity to "bear one another's burdens" in faithful, concerned visitation and counseling.

3. The pastor should be the master of his own personal schedule as far as possible. He will need to develop a strategy which will aid him in making the best use of his time.

4. An essential priority visitation and counseling schedule will include emergency calls, routine visits, and casual encounters.

5. As a general rule pastors have found it practical to reserve the morning hours for creative study and planning, the afternoon for visitation and counseling, and some of the evenings for essential committee and small group meetings in the church. It is understood that emergency cases may interrupt his schedule at any time.

6. Personal calling and counseling should be purposeful and specific. This will call for a certain preparation of spirit and of content materials, such as facts about the person to be visited or counseled, the choice of Scripture verses, guiding thoughts, and prayers to be used.

7. The art of interpersonal communication in a responsive relationship should be mastered if pastor and laity are to minister effectively to their fellowmen.

8. As a general rule, it is advisable to read the Bible and pray with troubled people. However, wise use should be made of Scripture reading, prayer, and counsel in keeping with the openness and responsiveness of the individual. No attempt should be made to force a person to respond.

Suggested Scriptures and Prayers

The following Scripture passages are arranged according to the various needs of persons. Some of these passages will fit more than one classification. A few are written out so that this manual may sometimes be adequate. The Bible may be preferred for use of longer passages. The prayers simply suggest purpose and scope and are not meant to be substituted for spontaneous prayers.

Thanksgiving for the Birth of a Baby
SCRIPTURE PASSAGES

Bless the Lord O my soul: and all that is within me, bless his holy name. Bless the Lord, O my soul, and forget not all his benefits [*Psalm 103: 1–2, KJV*].

He shall feed his flock like a shepherd: He shall gather the lambs with his arm, and carry them in his bosom, and shall gently lead those that are with young [*Isa. 40:11, KJV*].

Then children were brought to him that he might lay his hands on them and pray. . . . Jesus said, "Let the children come to me, and do not hinder them; for to such belongs the kingdom of heaven." And he laid his hands on them and went away [*Matt. 19:13–15, RSV*].

And Mary said, "My soul magnifies the Lord, and my spirit rejoices in God my Savior, for he has regarded the low estate of his handmaiden. . . . ; for he who is mighty has done great things for me, and holy is his name. And his mercy is on those

who fear him from generation to generation"
[*Luke 1:46–50, RSV*].

Other passages: Psalm 116:1–2,5–9,12–14,19; 127:
1,3; Matthew 18:1–6; Mark 10:13–16.

PRAYER

Eternal God, creator and father of us all, we
thank thee for the preservation of the life of this
mother and for the creation of this new life. We
thank thee for this home and for the privilege this
father and mother have of bringing new life into
the world.

Bless this baby with a strong body and mind.
May it bring joy to the home and strengthen the
ties which bind the family together. Guide A——
and B—— in the rearing of the child that he/
she may grow in wisdom and stature and in favor
with God and man, through Jesus Christ our Lord.
Amen.

For Family Visitation and Marriage Counseling
SCRIPTURE PASSAGES

Seek ye first the kingdom of God, and his righteousness; and all these things shall be added unto
you [*Matt. 6:33, KJV*].

Love . . . is slow to lose patience—it looks for

a way of being constructive. It is not possessive: it is neither anxious to impress nor does it cherish inflated ideas of its own importance. Love has good manners and does not pursue selfish advantage. It is not touchy. It does not keep account of evil or gloat over the wickedness of other people. On the contrary, it is glad with all good men when truth prevails. Love knows no limit to its endurance, no end to its trust, no fading of its hope; it can outlast anything. It is, in fact, the one thing that still stands when all else has fallen [*1 Cor. 13:4–8, Phillips**].

Be subject to one another out of reverence for Christ. Wives, be subject to your husbands, as to the Lord. For the husband is the head of the wife as Christ is the head of the church, his body, and is himself its Savior. As the church is subject to Christ, so let wives also be subject in everything to their husbands. Husbands, love your wives, as Christ loved the church and gave himself up for her . . . Even so husbands should love their wives as their own bodies. . . . For this reason a man shall leave his father and mother and be joined to his wife, and the two shall become one. . . . let each one of you love his wife as himself, and let

---

* From *The New Testament in Modern English,* © J. B. Phillips. Used with permission of The Macmillan Company.

the wife see that she respects her husband [*Eph. 5:21–33,RSV*].

Other passages: Exodus 20:1–17 (the Ten Commandments); Deuteronomy 6:4–9; Proverbs 3:3–8; Matthew 5:1–16 (the Beatitudes); Ephesians 6:1–4, 10–18. See other passages on the dedication of a new home.

PRAYER

Our heavenly Father, we praise thee for thy love on which the home was established. We thank thee for this home, for thy blessings upon it, and for the love on which it was begun. Now, O Lord, wilt thou grant grace and strength and wisdom to this father and mother [*A_____ and B_____*] as they share in their mutual responsibilities. Help them to grow in the grace and knowledge of Jesus Christ so that they may provide an example for their children and a ministry to the church and community, in the name of Christ our Lord. Amen.

For Those Who Are Ill

SCRIPTURE PASSAGES

God is our refuge and strength, a very present help in trouble. Therefore will not we fear, though the earth be removed, and though the mountains be carried into the midst of the sea; . . . Be still, and know that I am God: . . . The Lord of hosts is with us; the God of Jacob is our refuge [*Psalm 46:1–11,KJV*].

Cast thy burden upon the Lord, and he shall sustain thee: he shall never suffer the righteous to be moved [*Psalm 55:2,KJV*].

Wait on the Lord: be of good courage, and he shall strengthen thine heart: wait, I say, on the Lord [*Psalm 27:14,KJV*].

Come unto me, all ye that labour and are heavy laden, and I will give you rest. Take my yoke upon you, and learn of me; for I am meek and lowly in heart: and ye shall find rest unto your souls [*Matt. 11:28–29, KJV*].

Thou dost keep him in perfect peace, whose mind is stayed on thee, because he trusts in thee [*Isa. 26:3, RSV*].

Other passages: Psalm 27; 37:5–7,39; 91:1–4, 14–16; Isaiah 58:8; Lamentations 3:22–26; James 5: 15–16. For other appropriate passages see the list for general use given below.

PRAYER

Eternal God, our refuge and strength, thou art the Lord of life and health. We thank thee for all thy past mercies upon this thy servant [*A———*].

Let him now be aware of thy presence, and give him faith to trust thee for thy love and power, that he may receive health and salvation according to thy will. Grant him forgiveness of all his sins, strengthen him with thy goodness, and fill him with thy joy and peace. Guide the physician and the nurses who minister to him. Bless his family with thy gracious love. Teach us all to trust thee more implicitly, and keep us in thy loving care, through Jesus Christ our Lord. Amen.

For Those Suffering Pain

SCRIPTURE PASSAGES

I will lift up mine eyes unto the hills, from whence cometh my help. My help cometh from the Lord, which made heaven and earth. He will not suffer thy foot to be moved: he that keepeth thee will not slumber. . . . The Lord shall preserve thee from all evil: He shall preserve thy soul [*Psalm 121:1–7, KJV*].

They that wait upon the Lord shall renew their strength; they shall mount up with wings as eagles; they shall run, and not be weary; and they shall walk, and not faint [*Isa. 40:31, KJV*].

I consider that the sufferings of this present time are not worth comparing with the glory that is to be revealed to us. . . . the Spirit helps us in our weakness; for we do not know how to pray as we ought, but the Spirit himself intercedes for us with sighs too deep for words [*Rom. 8:18–26,RSV*].

My grace is sufficient for you, for my power is made perfect in weakness [*2 Cor. 12:9,RSV*].

Other passages: Job 2:7–10; 3:20–26; 23:3; 38:1–3; 42:1–6,10,12,17; Psalm 23; 27:14; 34:19–22; 40:1–3; 46; 91:1–2,4,15; Isaiah 26:3; 30:15; Matthew 11:28–29; Luke 22:41–43; John 14:27; 2 Corinthians 4:17–18; 12:7–10; James 1:2–4; 5:10–11,13–16; 1 Peter 5:6–7,10–11.

PRAYER

Merciful Father, thou who dost understand our suffering, we turn to thee in the time of our stress. Grant to thy servant [*A*——] strength to endure his pain. May he rely upon thy grace and not alone upon his own ability. Bless the hands that minister to him in this hour of need. Grant to all of us understanding, so that we may trust in the great Shepherd who suffered for us, even Jesus Christ our Lord. Amen.

For the Anxious and Fearful

SCRIPTURE PASSAGES

The Lord is my light and my salvation; whom shall I fear? the Lord is the strength of my life;

of whom shall I be afraid? . . . For in the time of trouble he shall hide me in his pavilion: in the secret of his tabernacle shall he hide me; he shall set me up upon a rock [*Psalm 27:1–5,KJV*].

Be gracious to me, O God, . . . When I am afraid, I put my trust in thee. In God, whose word I praise, in God I trust without a fear [*Psalm 56: 1–4,RSV*].

Why are you cast down, O my soul, and why are you disquieted within me? Hope in God; for I shall again praise him, my help and my God [*Psalm 42:11,RSV*].

Cast your burden on the Lord, and he will sustain you [*Psalm 55:22,RSV*].

He that dwelleth in the secret place of the most High shall abide under the shadow of the Almighty. . . . Thou shalt not be afraid for the terror by night; nor for the arrow that flieth by day; nor for the pestilence that walketh in darkness; nor for the destruction that wasteth at noonday. . . . For he shall give his angels charge over thee, to keep thee in all thy ways [*Psalms 91:1–11, KJV*].

The eternal God is thy refuge, and underneath are the everlasting arms [*Deut. 33:27, KJV*].

It is the Lord who goes before you; he will be with you, he will not fail you or forsake you; do not fear or be dismayed [*Deut. 31:8, RSV*].

Let not your hearts be troubled; believe in God, believe also in me. . . . Peace I leave with you; . . . Let not your hearts be troubled, neither let them be afraid [*John 14:1–27, RSV*].

Have no anxiety about anything, but in everything by prayer and supplication with thanksgiving let your request be made known to God. And the peace of God, which passes all understanding, will keep your hearts and your minds in Christ Jesus [*Phil. 4:6–7, RSV*].

Other passages: Psalm 24:4–8; 46:1; 42:1–11; 91:1–16; Proverbs 3:5–6; Isaiah 12:1–2; Matthew 6: 25–30; Romans 8:28.

PRAYER

Almighty God, we acknowledge thy strength and thy concern for us. Bestow thy mercy upon thy servant [A——] in his weakness and help-lessness. Give to him clarity of understanding. Deliver him from troubled and anxious thoughts and from conflicting and distressing emotions. Help him to put his mind on thee, and increase his faith, that he may trust thee implicitly. May the light of thy love shine clearly upon him, so that he may have peace and rest, in the name of Jesus Christ our Lord. Amen.

For Those Who Seek Forgiveness

SCRIPTURE PASSAGES

O Lord, thou hast searched me, and known me. Thou knowest my downsitting and mine uprising, thou understandest my thoughts afar off. . . . Search me, O God, and know my heart: try me, and know my thoughts: And see if there be any wicked way in me, and lead me in the way everlasting [*Psalm 139:1–24, KJV*].

Have mercy on me, O God, according to thy steadfast love; according to thy abundant mercy blot out my transgressions. Wash me thoroughly from my iniquity, and cleanse me from my sin! . . . Create in me a clean heart, O God, and put a new and right spirit within me. Cast me not away from thy presence, and take not thy holy Spirit from me. Restore to me the joy of thy salvation, and uphold me with a willing spirit [*Psalm 51:1–12, RSV*].

Come now, let us reason together, says the Lord: though your sins are like scarlet, they shall be as white as snow; though thy are red like crimson, they shall become like wool [*Isa. 1:18, RSV*].

Seek the Lord while he may be found, call upon him while he is near; let the wicked forsake his way, and the unrighteous man his thoughts; let him return to the Lord, that he may have mercy on him, and to our God, for he will abundantly pardon [*Isa. 55:6-7, RSV*].

If we confess our sins, he is faithful and just, and will forgive our sins and cleanse us from all unrighteousness [*1 John 1:9, RSV*].

If anyone does sin, we have an advocate with the Father, Jesus Christ the righteous; and he is the expiation for our sins, and not for ours only but also for the sins of the whole world [*1 John 2:1-2, RSV*].

Other passages: Psalm 32:1-2; 63:1-8; 101:1-3; 116; 130; 139:1-10, 23-24; 145; Isaiah 55:1-3; Matthew 5:23-24; 6:9-15; 11:28-30; Luke 15:1-7, 11-24: John 3:16-18; 1 John 2:9-11;4:7-11.

PRAYER

Our Father, thou who hast expressed thy forgiving love to us in the gift of thy Son Christ Jesus, we give thanks to thee for the promise of thy redemption. Thou who art always willing to forgive, blot out our transgressions. Forgive us for our disobedience to thy commands and our neglect of thee. Forgive our sins against our fellowman. Forgive us for evil thoughts and for allowing sin to dominate our minds. Wilt thou teach A—— how to surrender completely to thee and to open his life honestly before thee. Grant him the grace to accept thy forgiveness and love. Help him to accept himself as forgiven, and grant him the assurance of thy salvation. Confirm and strengthen him in his desire to live for thee and bring him to everlasting life, through Jesus Christ our Saviour. Amen.

For the Aged

SCRIPTURE PASSAGES

Lord, thou hast been our dwelling place in all generations. Before the mountains were brought forth, or ever thou hadst formed the earth and the world, even from everlasting to everlasting, thou art God. . . . O satisfy us early with thy mercy; that we may rejoice and be glad all our days. . . . Let thy work appear unto thy servants, and thy glory unto their children [*Psalm 90:1—17,KJV*].

Seeing we are compassed about with so great a cloud of witnesses, let us lay aside every weight, and the sin which doth so easily beset us, and let us run with patience the race that is set before us, looking unto Jesus the author and finisher of our faith; who for the joy that was set before him endured the cross, despising the shame, and is set down at the right hand of the throne of God [*Heb. 12:1–2,KJV*].

Eye hath not seen, nor ear heard, neither have entered into the heart of man, the things which God hath prepared for them that love him. But God hath revealed them unto us by his Spirit: for the Spirit searcheth all things, yea the deep things of God. . . . Now we have received, not the spirit of the world, but the Spirit which is of God; that we might know the things that are freely given to us of God [*1 Cor. 2:9–12,KJV*].

Other passages: Psalm 23; 46; 91; Isaiah 40: 28–31; John 14; 16; Romans 8:18–39; 1 Corinthians 4:16–18. See also passages for general use given below.

PRAYER

Our eternal Heavenly Father, thou who dost look upon time from the beginning to the end as a part of thy eternity, we thank thee for the years of our lives. We are grateful for all the blessings thou hast bestowed upon A____ during these many years. We acknowledge that life comes from thee and that it will return to thee in thine own good time. Help us to put our trust in thee from day to day, and fill our lives with good things. Help us to be faithful unto thee and commit ourselves to thy blessed will. Use the example of our lives and the testimony of our lips to be a blessing to others as long as we live upon this earth. Keep our minds focused upon eternal things, and increase our hope from day to day, in the name of Jesus Christ our Lord. Amen.

For Those Facing Death

SCRIPTURE PASSAGES

Behold, what manner of love the Father hath bestowed upon us, that we should be called the sons of God: . . . Beloved, now are we the sons of God, and it doth not yet appear what we shall be: but we know that, when he shall appear, we shall be like him; for we shall see him as he is [1 John 3:1–2, KJV].

For we know that if the earthly tent we live in is destroyed, we have a building from God, a house not made with hands, eternal in the heavens. . . . So we are always of good courage; we know that while we are at home in the body we are away from the Lord, for we walk by faith, not by sight. We are of good courage, and we would rather be away from the body and at home with the Lord [2 Cor. 5:1–8, RSV].

Jesus said, "I will not leave you comfortless: I will come to you. . . . Because I live, ye shall live also. . . . Peace I leave with you, my peace I give unto you: not as the world giveth, give I unto you. Let not your heart be troubled, neither let it be afraid [*John 14:18–27,KJV*].

Other passages: Psalm 23; 27; 116; 121; John 11: 25–26; 14:1–3; Romans 8:31–38; Revelation 21:1–4.

PRAYER

Our Heavenly Father, thou hast ever been our refuge and strength. Life is given by thee and returns unto thee. We pray now thy will to be done in the life of A———. Bless and keep him both in this life and in the life everlasting. Grant assurance and peace and rest unto thy faithful servant, through Jesus Christ our Lord. Amen.

For General Use

The following passages will be found suitable for general use and may be selected for the various situations listed above.

SCRIPTURES

Psalm 1; 8; 16; 23; 24; 27; 34; 37:3–6; 42; 46; 67; 73:21–26; 84; 90; 91; 95:1–7; 96; 100; 103; 111; 116; 119:1–3,9–12,33–34,105,165; 121; 138:7–8; 145; 146; 150

Proverbs 1:1–16; 2:1–8; 3:1–6; 4:20–27; 12:1–3

Isaiah 12; 26:1–9; 40:1–11,27–31; 43:1–3; 53; 55; 61:1–3

Matthew 5:1–16; 6:9–13,25–34; 7:7–12; 8:14–17; 9:18–31,35–38; 11:25–30

Mark 1:29–45; 5:21–43; 6:45–56; 10:35–45; 12: 28–34; 14:32–42

Luke 4:31–44; 5:12–26; 7:11–16; 9:28–43; 11: 9–13; 15:1–7; 24:13–16,27–35.

John 1:1–18; 3:1–21; 4:5–30; 5:24–25; 6:44–51; 8:1–11; 10:1–18; 11:1–6,17–45; 13:1–17; 14:1–17, 27; 15:1–17; 17; 20:19–23

Romans 5:1–11; 8:1–17,18–30,31–39; 10:1–4,8– 13; 12

1 Corinthians 1:18–25; 13; 15:10–22,51–58

2 Corinthians 1:3–7; 4:5–18; 5:11–21; 12:1–10

Galatians 2:20; 5:1,13–26; 6:1–10,14.

Ephesians 1:3–12,15–23; 2:1–10; 3:13–21; 4:1–7, 23–32; 6:10–20

Philippians 1:1–11; 2:1–11; 3:7–14; 4:4–8; 4:11– 13,19.

Colossians 1:9–18; 3:1–17

1 Thessalonians 4:13–18; 5:12–24

1 Timothy 1:12–17; 4:11–16

2 Timothy 1:7–14; 2:11–13,15,22–26; 3:14–17; 4: 1–8

Titus 2:11–15; 3:1–8

Hebrews 2:9–18; 4:9–16; 5:1–9; 5:12 to 6:12; 7: 25–28; 9:24–28; 10:10–25; 11:1–16; 12:1–2,6–7,11– 14, 22–29; 13:8,15,20–21.

James 1:2–6,12–17,22–27; 3:17–18; 4:3,6–10; 5: 13–20

1 Peter 1:3–9,13–25; 2:1–10,17,21–25; 3:14–18; 4:1,7–19; 5:1–11

2 Peter 1:2–11; 3:8–15,18

1 John 1:1–10; 2:1–6; 3:1–11,14,18,23–24; 4:7–21; 5:1–5,12–15

Revelation 3:10–13,19–22; 5:11–13; 7:9–17; 21:1–7; 21:22 to 22:7,12–14,17,20

PRAYER

Lord, make me an instrument of thy peace!
Where there is hatred, let me sow love;
Where there is injury, pardon;
Where there is doubt, faith;
Where there is despair, hope;
Where there is darkness, light;
Where there is sadness, joy.

O Divine Master, grant that I may not so much
    seek
To be consoled, as to console;
To be understood, as to understand;
To be loved, as to love.
For it is in giving that we receive;
It is in pardoning that we are pardoned;
It is in dying unto ourselves that we are born to
    eternal life.

ST. FRANCIS OF ASSISI

Part IX

Further Resources

The following information is provided as a ready reference for church leaders. It includes many items of practical value in planning for worship and special services and in ministering to people's needs, and discusses the Christian Year and Calendar, the church covenant, affirmations of faith, letters, certificates, and records.

The Christian Year and Church Calendar

An outline of the Christian Year should include certain traditional elements and also certain holidays and other special days which provide opportunity for emphasis in study and worship. Each church will determine which days it will emphasize. Since many churches begin the church year on October 1, the following calendar will be arranged in that manner. An asterisk appears beside the special seasons and days found in the traditional Christian Calendar.

October

Church Loyalty Season—an emphasis on teaching and training in church membership

Laymen's Sunday—third Sunday

Reformation Sunday—emphasis on the beginning of the Protestant Reformation, the last Sunday

November

Christian Stewardship Emphasis—enlistment in giving to the church

Dedication Day—subscribe church budget

Thanksgiving Sunday—the Sunday before Thanksgiving

Thanksgiving Day—fourth Thursday

*Season of Advent—from Advent Sunday through Christmas Eve; preparation for the coming of Christ

*Advent Sunday—fourth Sunday before Christmas; beginning of Christian Year Calendar; last Sunday in November or first Sunday in December

December

World (Foreign) Missions Emphasis

Universal Bible Sunday—second Sunday

*Christmas Sunday—Sunday before Christmas Day; emphasis on the Incarnation and hope of salvation in Jesus Christ

Christmas Day—December 25

Student Recognition Day—some Sunday during the Christmas holidays

January

New Year Sunday—Sunday before New Year's Day Emphasis on Bible study

*Epiphany Season—beginning January 6; emphasis on manifestation of Christ to the Gentiles as symbolized in the visit of the Magi

February

Christian World Fellowship Sunday—first Sunday

Race Relations Sunday—Sunday nearest February 12
Christian Education Emphasis—third or fourth Sunday

March

Home (National) Missions Emphasis—first or second
Sunday
*Lenten Season—beginning with Ash Wednesday and
continuing through Easter Eve; season of self-ex-
amination, penitence, and renewal
*Ash Wednesday—beginning of Lent, seventh week
before Easter
World Day of Prayer—first Friday in Lent, six weeks
before Good Friday
*Palm Sunday—Sunday before Easter; emphasis on the
triumphal entry of Christ
*Holy Week—week between Palm Sunday and Easter;
emphasis on the last acts of Jesus
*Maundy Thursday—inauguration of the Lord's Supper
*Good Friday—the day of the crucifixion
*Easter Sunday—commemorating the resurrection;
sometimes comes in March, sometimes in April; see
list of Easter Sundays on page 145

April

Emphasis on life commitment and Christian vocation
Emphasis on Christian stewardship
Life Commitment Sunday—last Sunday
*Pentecost—seventh Sunday or fifty days after Easter;
emphasis on the coming of the Holy Spirit and
Christian unity

May

National Christian Family Week—first full week in
May

Mother's Day—second Sunday, Christian home emphasis

Memorial Sunday—Sunday nearest May 30; memorial
service for those who have died during the past year

June

Emphasis on youth of the church—first or second
Sunday

Emphasis on Vacation Bible School

Father's Day—third Sunday

July

National Independence or Freedom Sunday—Sunday
before July 4

Emphasis on church encampments and Christian re-
creation

Emphasis on Christian literature—second Sunday

August

Emphasis on leadership enlistment for new church year

Emphasis on church library and reading

Emphasis on church retreats and renewal

September

Labor Sunday—the Sunday before the first Monday

Public Education and College Sunday—recognition of
opening of the public schools and young people's
entrance into college, second Sunday

Church Rally Day—third Sunday

Church Preparation Week—program planning, last week

Leadership Commitment Sunday—installation of church leaders, last Sunday

Easter Sundays from A.D. 1969 to 2012
(The years marked with an asterisk are Leap Years.)

1969 . . . April 6	1991 . . . March 31
1970 . . . March 29	*1992 . . . April 19
1971 . . . April 11	1993 . . . April 11
*1972 . . . April 2	1994 . . . April 3
1973 . . . April 22	1995 . . . April 16
1974 . . . April 14	*1996 . . . April 7
1975 . . . March 30	1997 . . . March 30
*1976 . . . April 18	1998 . . . April 12
1977 . . . April 10	1999 . . . April 4
1978 . . . March 26	*2000 . . . April 23
1979 . . . April 15	2001 . . . April 15
*1980 . . . April 6	2002 . . . March 31
1981 . . . April 19	2003 . . . April 20
1982 . . . April 11	*2004 . . . April 11
1893 . . . April 3	2005 . . . March 27
*1984 . . . April 22	2006 . . . April 16
1985 . . . April 7	2007 . . . April 8
1986 . . . March 30	*2008 . . . March 23
1987 . . . April 19	2009 . . . April 12
*1988 . . . April 3	2010 . . . April 4
1989 . . . March 26	2011 . . . April 24
1990 . . . April 15	*2012 . . . April 8

Church Covenants

A church covenant is a voluntary commitment of church members to give mutual care and support to one another and to work together in the ministry of the church. Any church may formulate its own covenant. A traditional covenant (I) and a contemporary one (II) are included here.

A Church Covenant (I)

Having been led, as we believe, by the Spirit of God, to receive the Lord Jesus Christ as our Saviour, and on the profession of our faith having been baptized in the name of the Father, and of the Son, and of the Holy Spirit, we do now in the presence of God, angels, and this assembly, most solemnly and joyfully enter into covenant with one another, as one body in Christ.

We engage, therefore, by the aid of the Holy Spirit, to walk together in Christian love; to strive for the advancement of this church, in knowledge, holiness, and comfort; to promote its prosperity and spirituality; to sustain its worship, ordinances, discipline, and doctrines.

To contribute cheerfully and regularly to the support of the ministry, the expenses of the church, the relief of the poor, and the spread of the gospel through all nations.

We also engage to maintain family and secret

devotion; to educate our children religiously; to
seek the salvation of our kindred and acquaintances;

To walk circumspectly in the world; to be just
in our dealings, faithful in our engagements, and
exemplary in our deportment; to avoid all tattling,
backbiting, and excessive anger; to abstain from
the sale and use of intoxicating drinks as a bever-
age; and to be zealous in our efforts to advance the
kingdom of our Saviour.

We further engage to watch over one another
in brotherly love; to remember each other in prayer;
to aid each other in sickness and distress; to
cultivate Christian sympathy in feeling and courtesy in speech; to be slow to take offense, but always ready for reconciliation and, mindful of the
rules of our Saviour, to secure it without delay.

We moreover engage that when we remove from
this place, we will as soon as possible unite with
some other church, where we can carry out the
spirit of this covenant and the principles of God's
Word.

A Church Covenant (II)

Having been led by the Spirit of God to receive
Jesus Christ as Saviour and Lord by faith, and
having publicly confessed him by baptism in the

name of God the Father, Son, and Holy Spirit, we freely and joyfully enter into covenant with one another as one body in Christ.

We pledge, therefore, by the aid of God's Spirit, to live together in Christian love; to work for the advancement of God's kingdom through this church in knowledge, holiness, and mutual care; to support its ministry by a faithful stewardship of money, time, and talents; and to sustain its worship, ordinances, doctrines, and disciplines.

We also pledge to maintain family and private worship, to rear our children in the nurture and spirit of the Lord; to seek the salvation of all members of our own families and of our acquaintances; and to strive for maturity in ourselves and in our fellow Christians.

We further pledge to follow Christian principles of morality in our daily living; to be ethical in our dealings and faithful in our commitments; to promote the unity of fellowship by proper attitudes and careful speech; and to be zealous in our efforts toward the advancement of the kingdom of God here and throughout the world.

Affirmations of Faith

Throughout Christian history churches have prepared forms of doctrinal statement known as creeds, confessions, articles, or affirmations of faith, setting forth the basic Christian beliefs. These have been adopted by the various churches as standards of doctrine for the instruction and unity of the people. They have also been used as an appeal in controversy. They are not held by many churches as binding the conscience or limiting the faith of individual believers except in certain major doctrines. The Bible alone is authoritative over the conscience of the individual and always takes precedence over the creeds and confessions of faith. A local church or other body of Christians may desire to write its own creed or confession of faith in light of the Bible and the historic creeds.

These various statements of faith include the Apostles' Creed, the oldest summary of Christian doctrine now in existence; the Nicene Creed, adopted by the Council of Nicea, A.D. 325; the Thirty-Nine Articles, constituting the confession of the Church of England; the Westminster Confession, the leading doctrinal expression of the Presbyterian churches; the New Hampshire Confession, adopted by the New Hampshire Baptist State Convention in 1830; the Philadelphia Confession, substantially that of the English Baptists, issued in London in 1689 and adopted in 1742 by the old Philadelphia Baptist Association; and the Articles of Faith of the Southern Baptist Convention adopted at Kansas City, 1962. The Apostles' Creed and a suggested contemporary affirmation of faith are included below as examples.

The Apostles' Creed (I)

I believe in God the Father Almighty, maker of

heaven and earth; and in Jesus Christ his only Son our Lord; who was conceived by the Holy Spirit, born of the virgin Mary, suffered under Pontius Pilate, was crucified, dead, and buried; the third day he rose from the dead; he ascended into heaven, and sitteth at the right hand of God the Father Almighty; from thence he shall come to judge the quick and the dead. I believe in the Holy Spirit, the holy catholic Church, the communion of saints, the forgiveness of sins, the resurrection of the body, and the life everlasting. Amen.

A Contemporary Affirmation of Faith (II)

We believe in God the Father, Creator and Ruler of all things, the source of all goodness, truth, and love;

We believe in Jesus Christ the Son, God manifest in the flesh, Redeemer and Lord, and everliving head of the church;

We believe in the Holy Spirit, God ever-present, for guidance, comfort, and strength;

We believe in the forgiveness of sins by God's grace, upon confession in repentance and faith;

We believe in the church as a fellowship of believers in Christ, established for the purpose of worship, ministry, and proclamation;

We believe in the kingdom of God as God's

sovereign rule in the life of man, in the brotherhood of man under the fatherhood of God, in the
final triumph of righteousness, and in the resurrection and the life everlasting. Amen.

Letter of Recommendation (Dismissal)

Dear Brethren,

This is to certify that ———— is a member of this
church in good and regular standing, and, that by his/
her own request is dismissed from our fellowship, for
the purpose of uniting with you.

May the blessing of God rest on him/her and you
as you serve our Lord together.

Done by the order of the ———————— church,

———————, 19—.

Signed ————————, Clerk.

License of a Minister

This is to certify that ———— is a member of the
———————— church, in good and regular standing. We
believe he has been called of God to the work of the
gospel ministry, and do hereby give him our approval
in the performance of his ministry toward the maturity
of his gifts, as God may provide the opportunity. We
pray that God may endow him with grace and patience
and steadfastness as he matures and proves himself in
the ministry.

Done by order of the church ————, 19—.

————, Pastor.

————, Clerk.

Certificate of Ordination for Ministers

This certifies that ———was publicly set apart to
the work of the gospel ministry, with prayer and the
laying on of hands, by the approval of the ————
church, and according to the practices of our denomination, at ———, ———, 19—.

We pledge to him the support of our prayers and
our cooperation as he enters upon the work of the
ministry, performing all of the duties and assuming
the responsibilities included in the work of a Christian
minister in the church of our Lord Jesus Christ.

(The certificate should be signed by appropriate officers of the church and may be signed by other parti-
cipants.)

The Minister's Records

The minister's records, if faithfully kept, can aid in
the efficiency of his work and provide a history of his
own ministry, the persons served, and the entire church's
ministry. A filing system should include classification
of his library, a record of worship services, sermons
preached, baptisms administered, weddings, funeral services, special dedication services, visitation and counseling, his own family anniversaries, and significant community activities.

A filing system for his library.—Indexing according
to subjects is recommended for the minister's library.
This is outlined in L. R. Elliott, *The Efficiency Filing
System* (Nashville: Broadman Press, 1950). Some ministers use a modified form of the Dewey decimal system
commonly used in public libraries. A 3 by 5 card

subject index may be made of all books and other entries of importance. Baker Book House, Grand Rapids, Michigan, provides a system which includes the various needs of the minister's filing system in one book.

Record for weddings.—The minister should keep a record of all marriage ceremonies performed, giving the date, the names of the couple, the place of the wedding, and the witnesses. A simple notebook may be arranged to include these.

Record of funerals.—The record of funerals should include the date, the name and age of the individual, the place where the service was held, and any note of interest which the minister desires to keep.

Special records.—The minister may wish to keep a record of special occasions and significant ministries in a notebook provided for that purpose. This should probably be kept for private use only, especially certain occasions in private counseling.

Important Addresses

Important addresses of denominational institutions and agencies, as well as headquarters of other churches, may be valuable. The pastor may want to have on hand the two given below:

Executive Committee
Southern Baptist Convention
460 James Robertson Parkway
Nashville, Tennessee 37219

The Sunday School Board
Southern Baptist Convention
127 Ninth Avenue, North
Nashville, Tennessee 37203
                    (Headquarters for
                    publication of books
                    and literature)

Each minister may write in the addresses of certain
leaders and the headquarters of his own denomination.

The National Council of Churches, 475 Riverside
Drive, New York, New York 10027, can provide information concerning various denominations, the ecu-
menical movement, Christianity and world issues, and
much valuable literature of use to Christians generally.